AF230422

# ARROWS

RAISING CHILDREN TO HIT
THEIR GOD-GIVEN MARK

KEELEY SCHAFER

*Like arrows in the hand of a warrior,*
*so are the children of one's youth.*

—P S A L M 127:4 (N A S )

# CONTENTS

# FOREWORD

What is really cool about this book is that it is the culmination of a lot of struggles and mistakes made easy by the correction, application and declaration of the Word of God! From my perspective, it has been a remarkable journey to live with, grow with, and raise children with this woman. From the day I met her until this moment, she has been determined that the things of God would be the center of our family.

We have learned to not just raise our children, declare over them, expect more from them, and push them toward their God-given talents and gifts but to honor them for who God created them to be. Psychology today may tell you it is difficult dealing with sibling rivalry and that birth order affects outcome, but the principles laid out in God's Word are timeless and second to none, and will work in any generation.

Although we attribute our success to our parents and pastors who endured struggles, equipped us to have a successful marriage and raise godly children, there is one pivotal moment I believe that was key to all of this coming together. The moment a woman (my mother-in-law, Darla Stookey) decided that enough was enough, took a stand, and determined in her heart that her family would be in church. It would not just be any church, but a church with a firm foundation founded and standing to this day on God's Word! That day of decision began a chain of cataclysmic destruction that declared war on the kingdom of hell!! Thank you, Mom, for without that moment none of us would be here.

Since I have lived out the stories and am one of the characters in this book, I feel like the life we have lived over the past thirty-two years was the movie. And if you are an avid reader you know how the saying goes, "the book is better than the movie!"

—KEVIN SCHAFER

*Keeley's husband*

As an arrow that has been shot into the world with prayer, support, and trust, I am blessed to have been raised in the quiver of Kevin and Keeley Schafer. I hark back to a distinct memory from my childhood, around the age of seven or eight years. Sitting in the back of my mother's black, 2000 Ford Windstar, traveling southbound past Gateway High School on Mosside Boulevard in Monroeville, PA, I remember watching the road ahead diligently. As a car-obsessed child (thanks to my dad), I asked, "Mom, when will I be able to drive?" She kindly replied, "When you turn sixteen!" Doing some elemental calculation in my head I excitedly responded, "That's about eight years, Mom! That's not that long!" After I had exclaimed my enthusiasm of someday conquering the open road, there was a hesitation before my mother's next words. I believe in that moment she experienced a heavenly pause—a reflection of the present and a glimpse of the future for her and her child. "You're right, Bud," she said. "It's not that long." The age of sixteen eventually came and went. Roads in my town were conquered. Then eighteen and twenty. As I write this, I am twenty-two years of age and now realize the wisdom in my mother's response. I could not tell you exactly what she heard or the emotions she felt in that moment years ago, but I do know that the next "quick" eight years and beyond were filled with love, compassion, patience, failure, success, tears, laughter, prayer, and worship. Through it all God's Word was held paramount.

It was the cornerstone of everything we did and did not do. No, I didn't get to see "that" movie with all my friends. No, I wasn't allowed to talk to my parents "like that." Yes, I did get that spanking in the mall parking lot while bystanders thought both my parents and I were insane. And I am grateful for all of it. In those moments of discipline, I was always reminded that the decisions my parents made came from a place of love. That consistency is what I admire about my mother and my father.

I am in college now and yes, I live differently than most! My faith has been and continues to be tested in every aspect of my life, yet the hope I have in my Heavenly Father is what sets me apart from the crowd. I declare that I am a living testimony of Deuteronomy 5:16, "Honor your father and your mother, as the Lord your God has commanded you, that your days may be long, and that it may be well with you in the land which the Lord your God is giving you." The Lord has opened up some pretty special opportunities for me in the past few years. My parent's reverence for God's Word coupled with the moral foundations they laid prepared me for those very opportunities. Had they not parented the way they did, standing strong in their beliefs and not succumbing to the norms of society, I would not be the man I am today. Thank you, Mom and Dad.

—AUSTIN SCHAFER
*Keeley and Kevin's son (22 years old)*

I remember my mom came home a few years ago saying that a lady at church had told her to write a book about parenting. I laughed to myself and thought, "Why? What's so special about us?" Looking back at my childhood, I now realize just how different my experience was from other kids. Yes, there were many similarities in the way I was raised when compared to my friends or kids I went to school with. But, I do remember MANY nights staying at home while my friends were out because my parents did not let me go see a particular movie or go to a haunted house with them, just to name a few. On those nights, I was not the happiest camper, but I don't think I fully understood exactly why my parents did what they did. Their choices weren't because they didn't want me to have fun; my mom and dad based all of their parenting on biblical principles. Their reason was never "because I said so." It was always "because the Bible says so." I think that's the most important thing to grasp from this book. Raising your children is not about doing what you think is the right thing; it's always about using biblical truths in every aspect of your child's life. My parents weren't just Christians at church—they were Christians at home, too. I was surrounded by scripture my entire life. I even find myself repeating the same verses my parents would so often say throughout my childhood. My mom and dad raised me and my siblings to be loving, bold, God-fearing people. They disciplined us when it was needed and encouraged us to do what we were passionate about. I know that whoever reads this book will receive some incredible wisdom on how to raise a child. My mom is an AMAZING woman, and I believe that this book will not only help your children grow and become better, but I pray that as a result, YOU become better, too. May God bless you in your endeavor to become a Spirit-filled, kind, and wise parent!

—KAMRYN SCHAFER
*Keeley and Kevin's daughter (19 years old)*

Growing up with my parents, there was definitely a lot to learn and receive from them. There really was not a day that went by where you couldn't learn something from my parents. Every time I was disciplined, I remember both of them telling me "you're gonna thank me one day." Of course, being the stubborn child I was at the time, I rolled my eyes behind their back and walked upstairs calmly just so I could make it to my room to think on all these restrictions—whether it was from a tv show or even a boy—and how I was actually going to thank them later for everything. One day, the same routine happened. I got mad, faked my way up the stairs and made it to my secret place, thinking about why my parents would ever keep me from what I wanted so bad. But this time it was different. I experienced my first heartbreak. If you know teenage heartbreak, you know your mind is going all over the place. This was the first day I thanked them in my heart for all their care and provision. After that, I was able to look into every area of my life and start applying what my parents were telling me. Just like the Bible says, "Above all else, guard your heart, for everything you do flows from it" (Proverbs 4:23). Instead of sneaking around my parents' backs to be with that guy or listen to that music I know is not good for my spirit, I started to gain that discernment within myself. Everything my parents taught me was straight from a book called the Bible. I realized every time I rolled my eyes at them, I was rolling my eyes towards Heaven. God does not want us to be led of this world but wants us to be led by His Holy Spirit. If you noticed, I did not say my mom gave me the discernment of the Holy Spirit. Because of the way she raised me, I have been able to dwell on these areas in my life and have the urge inside to discover who the Holy Spirit is for myself. I believe the same can happen for you and your kids.

—DELANEY SCHAFER
*Keeley and Kevin's daughter (18 years old)*

Bringing into parenting my unresolved childhood trauma, coupled with thinking that a deep love for my child would automatically make me a great parent, was a recipe for disaster. It is by the healing, redeeming grace of our God that Keeley is the amazing woman she is today. Two good decisions can change the destiny of your family. Get God involved first and foremost, then read this book for wise and practical parenting guidance. Know better . . . do better.

—DARLA STOOKEY

*Keeley's mom*

The Schafer Family (left to right): Austin, Keeley, DeLaney, Kamryn, Kevin

# PREFACE

God has blessed me and my husband, Kevin, with three wonderful children. From day one, we had a strategy of how we would raise our children in the admonition of the Lord. As they grew and the fruit of their lives began to appear, we started receiving compliments from others on our parenting skills. We were honored to have received such words of affirmation but soon realized that many parents did not have a clear plan on how to raise their children. When I neared fifty years of age, I began sensing a tremendous weight to put into writing some of the things God had taught me about parenting. My first priority was to provide a parenting resource for my children, grandchildren, and future generations in my family. To be able to speak to my family, even when I'm in Heaven, gives me great satisfaction and peace. God broadened my focus to not only my family, but to other parents who need this vital information.

I believe this book contains the spiritual truths and practical guidelines to bring up successful, God-loving children. I believe God has anointed these pages to be a voice on the earth at this time and hour. I believe this book will equip parents to equip the next generation of world changers. May our arrows be mighty on the earth!

—KEELEY SCHAFER

# ARROWS MUST BE CRAFTED WITH PRECISION

It was 1978, in the heat of a West Texas summer, when my parents sat my younger sister and me down to explain they were parting ways and getting a divorce. We barely had time to process this heart-wrenching revelation when we were barreled over by another one. My dad took a deep breath and said, "Your mother and her college sweetheart from Indiana have reconnected and she is going to marry him. You girls are going to be moving to Indiana with her." From that point on all I heard was a jumble of words as my mind began to reel. Dad explained how exciting it was going to be for us. My soon-to-be stepfather had a dairy farm and we were going to have loads of fun. We would visit Dad a couple weeks in the summer and during the Christmas holiday. We could call him any time we wanted. He was doing his best to sell us on the benefits of this decision, but it was more than a nine-year-old little girl could take. In a matter of ten minutes I learned my parents were getting a divorce, my mom was marrying someone else, and we were moving over a thousand miles away!

Our house in Texas soon sold and my mother moved to Indiana to ready the trailer home we were going to live in while my parents' divorce was finalized. My sister and I stayed with my dad the last few weeks of summer. Those days were full of quality time, making memories, and spending some moments with Dad's relatives in Oklahoma. All too soon, the day came when it was time to go. My mom and her new boyfriend drove from Indiana to Oklahoma to pick us up, and we agreed to rendezvous at an area hotel restaurant. In walked my mom with the biggest smile on her face, linked arm in arm with the new guy she loved. It was the first time I had ever seen her with any other man than my father. It was one of the hardest days of my life.

We headed out and had been on the road for many hours. It was the middle of the night and most little girls would be fast asleep by then. Oh, how I wanted to sleep! The emotions of the day had taken their toll on me, but my aching heart would not allow it. All I could see were images of my dad—our last hug, his last kiss upon my cheek, and his last words ringing in my ears. My mind echoed with the multitude of "lasts" over the past month. Feeling the warm, sweaty cheek of my sleeping little sister leaning against my arm, I pondered the new life ahead of me. "Will I like Indiana? Will I make any friends? Will this sadness ever go away?"

Listening to the endless, whirring drone of the tires spinning on the road, I sat in the darkness, quiet and taking it all in. In front of me were the two silhouettes of my mother and her boyfriend glued to each other at the shoulders. This had been their standard position from the moment we left Oklahoma. I am sure they thought I was sleeping soundly when they began to kiss. It wasn't a "peck on the lips" kind of thing. This was an all-in, no holds barred, make-out session while my stepfather-to-be drove down the highway. I sat there horrified at the sight of my mother passionately kissing a man who just a few hours ago was a mere stranger in my eyes. I tried my hardest to muffle the unstoppable whimpers beginning to pour from my insides. It wasn't long before my mom spun around, leaned back over the seat, got as close to my face as possible, and in a confused whisper asked, "What's wrong with you?" As quietly as I could muster and pointing directly at her boyfriend, I responded, "You are kissing that man!" Her face wrinkled with irritation as she retorted, "That man is going to be my husband, so you'd better get used to it!" With one fluid movement, she whirled around and resumed her shoulder-to-shoulder position, but this time inching in closer than ever before while thrusting her head into the crook of his neck.

Suddenly, the world became eerily silent. I sat there in shock as a looming thought slowly oozed into the crevices of my mind, "I am alone." I squeezed my arm tightly around my sleeping little sister who was blissfully unaware of the circumstances. I wiped my eyes with a stoic resolve, realizing I had no one left to see my pain.

As I grew up, instead of allowing that pain to thrust me into an endless cycle of grief and loss, it became the catalyst in desiring a better life for my future children. I never wanted them to experience the agony of watching a marriage disintegrate, or the sting of feeling completely and utterly alone.

I know it was never my parents' intention to hurt me. They were only operating with the knowledge they had at the time. My mother was saved as a little girl, but she strayed from the Lord during my early childhood years. Thankfully, she returned to Him in full force and led me to the Lord when I was eight years old. My father and stepfather did not know Jesus at all until they were much older. I am sure if my parents had the chance to do it all over again, they would do things much differently. They did not have the strong foundation of Christ my husband and I did when we first got married. We were well ahead of the curve by having a godly game plan for parenting from day one.

My husband, Kevin, and I chose to learn from our parents' mistakes and allow any pain we experienced to push us forward. The wisdom of God helped us process the knowledge— good and bad—received from our backgrounds and apply it in a positive way. We were able to navigate how best to raise our children by allowing wisdom to reveal what to do and what NOT to do. We do not purport to be perfect parents, but with God's guidance we have raised three successful, God-loving children.

In Ephesians 6:10-12, we are encouraged to put on the full armor of God to stand against the enemy's tactics. It is clear that our battle is not against natural forces but against a spiritual foe we cannot see with our natural eyes.

> *Finally, be strong in the Lord and in his mighty power. Put on the full armor of God, so that you can take your stand against the devil's schemes. For our struggle is not against flesh and blood, but against the rulers, against the authorities, against the powers of this dark world and against the spiritual forces of evil in the heavenly realms. Therefore, put on the full armor of God, so that when the day of evil comes, you may be able to stand your ground, and after you have done everything, to stand. Stand firm then, with the belt of truth buckled around your waist, with the breastplate of righteousness in place, and with your feet fitted with the readiness that comes from the gospel of peace. In addition to all this, take up the shield of faith, with which you can extinguish all the flaming arrows of the evil one. Take the helmet of salvation and the sword of the Spirit, which is the word of God.*
>
> —Ephesians 6:10-12 (NIV)

The belt, the breastplate, the foot protection, the shield, the helmet, and the sword mentioned are all pieces that cover the body, or are weapons held in proximity to the person standing against the attacks of the enemy. In this passage, we see the devil uses flaming arrows in his advances against us. A battle game changer for us would be to have our own arrows that we could launch to obliterate enemy targets. The good news is that as parents, we have those arrows!

"Like arrows in the hand of a warrior, so are the children of one's youth" (Psalm 127:4, NAS).

Our children are the only weapons we have that can be launched into other generations to eradicate the enemy's effectiveness. Our children have the ability to stand firm in the truth of Christ long after we have passed away. What a tremendous advantage God has given us!

The process of creating an arrow to the final culmination of it hitting its target is a meticulous one. In order to maximize the effectiveness of our arrows, parenting can't be hit-and-miss. The cross-our-fingers-and-hope-for-the-best method is not a good plan. Therefore, parenting must be done with purpose and great precision.

Imagine grabbing a crooked, little, dried out twig off the ground and placing it in a bow to shoot a target hundreds of yards away. Most likely the stick would break into pieces as the string of the bow was pulled back. Even if it made it out of the bow, it would probably twirl and hit the ground a few feet ahead, sorely missing the intended destination. Arrows can't be haphazardly thrown together and expected to soar through the air to accurately hit a marked objective. In order to do so, they must be formed for precision with intentionality.

As parents, we realized the magnificent responsibility God had given us in the crafting and fine-tuning process of raising our children. Of course, we experienced challenges along the way, but they only reinforced the importance of arrows in the making.

## Hand-Picked Parents

I remember holding my newborn son, Austin. This was a day I had dreamed of for a very long time. I was finally a mother! I loved my son and felt an overwhelming responsibility to take care of him, but nothing could have ever prepared me for the sheer exhaustion I was about to experience. Days and nights were squashed together as I walked around in a sleep-deprived state. Highlights of my routine were feeding the baby, bathing the baby, changing the baby's diaper, changing the baby's clothes, and rocking the baby to sleep. These responsibilities consumed my world with little else that I could add to my plate. Just a month prior, I was sitting at a desk at an international corporation typing notes from a meeting regarding a multi-million-dollar contract. Going from an executive assistant to a stay-at-home mom was a huge shock! There were no more bonuses or accolades about what a great job I was doing. My life was defined by small things, which to most seemed very mundane. My identity took a great hit as my big world shrunk to the boundaries of my four walls. Several months after my son's birth, I experienced severe post-partum depression and irrationally began imagining ways to either take my life or run away to never be found again. Thankfully, I had the wherewithal to see a counselor and was put on medication for a temporary period of time which helped me get back on track again. If we have to take medication or are taking medication for any type of depression, we should not feel condemned. God will use whatever it takes to bring healing and clarity to our lives.

It took a while for me to wrap my head around my new normal as a parent. God allowed me to see how important it was to be my children's mother. Our children ultimately belong to God, but He gave Kevin and me the awesome responsibility to raise them. What an honor that He trusted us. It reminds me of what God said about Abraham soon after he told him Sarah would be having a baby.

"For I have chosen him, so that he will direct his children and his household after him to keep the way of the LORD by doing what is right and just, so that the LORD will bring about for Abraham what he has promised him" (Genesis 18:19, NIV).

Like Abraham and Sarah, we were hand-picked by God to be our children's parents because we will direct them in His ways!

As parents we have the opportunity to be the greatest influence, next to the Lord, on our children. It is not our job to make sure our children think we are the coolest parents on earth. Our greatest endeavor isn't to be their best bud and have a tag-along pal wherever we go. Our assignment as parents is to work alongside our Heavenly Father—the master arrow craftsman—to develop the qualities they need to thrive and excel as His sons and daughters.

## The Pressure of Comparison

In the process of raising children, it may be easy to check out everyone else's kids and parenting methods to see how we measure up. It seemed like as soon as my first child was born, I went into the comparative mom mode. How much does your child weigh? What percentile are they in? How much are they eating per day? Are they sleeping through the night? Are they eating solid food? Are they crawling? Are they walking? I would make the necessary calculations in my mind to see if my children were excelling, and God forbid if I felt they were coming up short in any area.

As my children got older, the comparisons were even more intense. Are your children going to preschool? Do they know all their colors? Do they know all their numbers? I was in awe of the moms whose days were perfectly planned with Pinterest- worthy festivities. Crafts, finger painting, picnics in the park, and frequent adventures at the museum were the status quo.

Then there was me. I felt like I was just trying to get by. I had three little ones with the oldest being four and the youngest being a few months old. The biggest feats I could muster were getting to the grocery store and to church. I used to beat myself up thinking I wasn't a good mom, "Look at Suzie and my friend, Molly, and their kids. They seem to be so happy and satisfied." "Look at my kids. They are obviously stunted. I'm not giving them all they need." I somehow muddled through those early years spending my energy on keeping my children clean, fed, and safe. Of course, we had some fun, but in my mind, I wasn't "mom of the year" material.

Fast forward twenty years, with God's help my kids have grown into wonderful young adults. They love the Lord and are serving Him. They are leaders in their schools and churches. They are rich in relationships. They turned out FINE! In retrospect, I now understand I was the perfect mom for my children and I see the fruits of my labor. I put myself through a lot of heartache and unnecessary pressure in the early days of mother - hood by comparing myself to other mothers.

We must come to grips that in certain seasons of child-raising we may have to cut out different committees, outside activities, and hobbies to focus on our children. We won't be able to maintain everything we did in order for our children to flourish. Our home may not be as spotless as it once was as we raise our young family. Hebrews 12:9-11 (ERV) says, "Without oxen a stable stays clean, but you need a strong ox for a large harvest". If we are blessed with children, our homes are full of extra life which means more dishes, laundry, and more dust! This scripture points out that we can have a clean stable as long as we don't have animals using it. A little "poo" in the stable comes with the territory when we're focused on the harvest. We must learn to hit the high spots and don't stress if our home isn't in pristine condition. Let's enjoy our children while they're little. They will be old enough to help us clean in the snap of a finger!

Galatians 6:4 (TLB) says, "Let everyone be sure to do his very best, for then he will have the personal satisfaction of work done well and won't need to compare himself with someone else." If we fix our gaze on the Lord and His guidance, we won't get sidetracked by looking at others. God has given us our very own special grace to raise our children.

Embracing the uniqueness of our children as well as our own parenting style is an important key in God's arrow designing process. Let's not get caught in the comparison trap. We don't need to raise our children like anyone else. We can be okay with that.

**Can I Ever Do Enough?**
With all of the pressure to compare myself as a parent, there also came a lot of second-guessing. Was I doing enough for my children? Could I do more? Could I do better? I began to poll some older, godly, spiritual women I respected whose children were successful adults. I asked each one of these amazing women if they ever felt like they did enough when it came to raising their children. Every single one of them said "NO!" These women have wonderful

children who are serving the Lord, and some of their children are in full-time ministry. I think feelings of inadequacy are something we all have to deal with as parents, especially moms. We can't do this thing on our own. We have to look to the Heavenly Father and remind ourselves it is not by our might and power but by the spirit of the living God (Zechariah 4:6).

Kevin and I had the privilege of attending Rhema Bible Training Center in Broken Arrow, OK. Pastor Kenneth Hagin, Jr. enforced in our ministry training that the natural coming together with the supernatural makes an explosive force for God. We should never discount all the small decisions, small adjustments, words of affirmation and encouragement given to our children day by day. God multiplies our limited human efforts with the infusion of His supernatural power. In the future, we'll look back and see all the progress made. When we feel overwhelmed or unequipped, 2 Corinthians 12: 9-10 (TPT) says:

> *My grace is sufficient for you, for My strength is made perfect in weakness. Therefore most gladly I will rather boast in my infirmities, that the power of Christ may rest upon me. Therefore I take pleasure in infirmities, in reproaches, in needs, in persecutions, in distresses, for Christ's sake. For when I am weak, then I am strong.*

This is God's perfect recipe for beautifully crafted arrows. Be encouraged! Christ in us is MORE THAN ENOUGH!

## Discipline

Disgruntled over his fifteen-year-old daughter's scathing Facebook post about him and her mother, a father decided to upload his own video post to Facebook. Calling out his daughter's name, he read her post aloud and began to harshly critique all of her arguments against him and his wife. He spoke directly into the camera as if his daughter were standing right there and cut her down to the best of his ability. He then took a gun and started blowing holes into his daughter's computer, putting an abrupt stop to any further internet activity. The post ended up going viral and five years later has over 41 MILLION views! A flood of thousands of "likes" proved many people believed this man's parenting efforts were heroic. Moreover, it proved how many people in society do not have a clear understanding of godly discipline.

Humiliation is never a proper way to discipline children. Humiliation actually says, "I don't respect you." If anyone should have their child's back, it is the parent. It is not funny to post a child's mistakes and they should NEVER be broadcast to the public. Proverbs 12:23 (ISV) says, "A prudent man keeps what he knows to himself, but the hearts of fools shout forth their foolishness." When a parent puts their child on display through social media to teach them a lesson, it actually reveals the extreme foolishness of the parent instead. Let's place ourselves in our children's shoes. Would we want our screw-ups announced to 41 million people? I think we all know the answer to that one. Parenting in this way is not creative or witty. It is abusive.

We've all heard parents yelling at their children in a restaurant, grocery store, or other public place. We've witnessed them calling them crude names, cursing at them, and demeaning them beyond belief. Some of these uncontrolled emotional outbursts are from parents who feel their children's behavior made them look bad, and their bullying tirade gives them a sense of revenge. We've seen the overwhelming embarrassment in the faces of young children who are three, four, and five years old, knowing they are being called out in front of a crowd of onlookers. Actions like these are just another form of humiliation guised in the deception of "this is what a good parent does."

Kevin and I have always been firm believers in private discipline. If we were at Wal-Mart, Chuck E. Cheese, a grocery store, or any public place, and our kids started acting up, we were quick to take them to the restroom or back to the car to discipline them. It was almost never convenient to do so, but in order to protect our children's dignity and maximize the discipline process, that's what we would do.

We spanked our children but never with our hands. Hands were made to love and embrace. Belts, switches off trees, or anything that would "whip" a child were off-limits. We used special wooden paddles with a handle that was about twelve inches long and about one inch thick to spank our children. The paddle was always an arm's reach away—one at home, one in each car, and one in my purse.

Spanking children when we're angry is never a good idea. Yelling, screaming, and letting our emotions take control are not effective ways to discipline. Rushing in and repeatedly spanking a child is scary for them, borders on abuse, and is not productive. Always take time to get a breather, calm down, and be in control! That's not easy to do in the heat of the moment. To be totally transparent, in the height of frustration I have had a few thoughts enter my mind to physically harm my children just to get them to be quiet or end the disobedient behavior. When I read the headlines about parents who abuse their children or kill them in a state of rage, I understand how it happened. They yielded to the same thoughts that crossed my mind. When we are especially tired or overwhelmed by stressful situations, negative ideas like these can be magnified. If we encounter these internal suggestions, we should not feel condemned. Those feelings don't just pop into our head accidentally. They were planted there by the devil himself. John 10:10 (TLB) says that the thief's purpose is to steal, kill and destroy. He is hoping we will act on that thought! The good news is we have the ability and strength through Christ to not give in to destructive thoughts.

> *We can demolish every deceptive fantasy that opposes God and break through every arrogant attitude that is raised up in defiance of the true knowledge of God. We capture, like prisoners of war, every thought and insist that it bow in obedience to the Anointed One.*
>
> —2 Corinthians 10:3-5 (TPT)

If a destructive thought to seriously harm our children enters our mind, we can command it to bow its knee to the obedience of Jesus Christ! We should take a breather, get our head together, and not be swayed by the devil's whispered intentions.

Our children should have an understanding of why they are being disciplined before we spank them. We should also give them an example in God's Word of why their actions were wrong. For example, if our daughter, DeLaney, hit her sister, Kamryn, we would handle it in this way. We would take her into a private area and say, "DeLaney, do you understand why you are going to be disciplined?" We would listen for the answer. We would then say, "Hitting your sister wasn't right. It hurt her and even if you felt like she did something wrong to you first, you should have kept control of yourself. God wants us to love our family, even when it's hard. The Bible says that we need to love one another just as Jesus loved us. I'm going to give you a spanking today and I believe that next time your sister makes you mad, you are going to make a better choice." If one of our children spoke unlovingly to us or disobeyed us, we would say, "The Word of God says to honor your father and mother because it is the first commandment with a promise.

God said if you honor us, you will live a long time and things will go well with you (Ephesians 6:3). Do you want to live a long time? Do you want things to go well with you?" Of course, their answers were always "yes." Our children can vouch that this scripture was used multiple times! Children need to understand that when they disobey, it isn't about letting us down as their parents, it's about them not honoring the Word of God. If we always point them back to the Word, they will adjust their behaviors based on God's truth and not just because we said so. This will establish a habit of them looking to God's Word for correction and guidance in their adult lives.

Prior to spanking, children should stand and either hold on to the back of a chair or bend over slightly while touching the edge of a mattress. We should aim for the mid-buttocks—the meatiest part—and not anywhere else on the body. We should never spank a child's bare bottom, out of respect for them and also for safety reasons. Usually one stroke will be sufficient, but we should never spank more than three times in a row. Proverbs 22:15 (KJV) says, "Foolishness is bound in the heart of a child, but the rod of correction shall drive it far from him." In David and Roxanne Swann's book *Guarantee Your Child's Success*, they explain this scripture with great insight. "I want you to get a new image in your mind – a Biblical picture – of what transpires when you correct your child God's way. As you discipline with the rod of correction, the Lord drives out foolishness and replaces it with His wisdom. I've seen parents get so angry they tried to drive the foolishness out of their child by swinging the rod so hard, they'd drive their child's head through sheet rock. It's not the strength of the parent's stroke, but in the strength of the parent's heart… The tool, the rod, is important, but it's more important how you use the rod and in what spirit you use it to impact the behavior of your children." What a comfort it is knowing God is doing a work in our children's hearts as we lovingly correct them His way.

We should immediately hold our child after a spanking and hug them as they cry. It is important that they feel comforted in the fact that we are not angry with them nor will we shun them for their actions. We should never banish our children after disciplining them by saying "Go to your room and get out of my sight!" God certainly would never do that to us. After he or she has settled down, have them take a moment to pray and ask the Lord to forgive them for what they did. When they are younger, it is easier for them to repeat a simple prayer we pray for them. If their disobedience impacted another individual, they should ask that individual's forgiveness. If it was a sibling and after their professed apology, children will usually hug and keep on playing like nothing ever happened. Once the discipline process is completed, we should not bring up their disobedient actions again. Drop it! Children have the right to experience God's full forgiveness and grace, just as much as we would want for ourselves.

Siblings will sometimes be inquisitive as to why their brother or sister got into trouble. We should never share our children's wrongdoings with their siblings. If our children ask about their brother or sister's spanking, we should say, "That is none of your business. Do you want us to share with brother or sister when you do something wrong? What happened is private between us and brother or sister, and you don't have to worry about it." A great respect will form between children as they give each other space to get things right without having to know all the things that went wrong.

Consistency is extremely important in discipline. If our children can't jump on the couch, then they should not be allowed to jump on the couch when we are tired and don't want to deal with it. We found when we were consistent about something every single time, the bad behavior was nipped in the bud before we knew it, because the kids realized mom and dad were serious about it. We frustrate our children when they can act out a bad behavior one day and the next day they can't. When we have multiple children, it is so easy to let things slide. Sometimes we think as long as they aren't hurting themselves or each other, are alive, and are fed and well, then it's all good. We can train ourselves to tune out certain things like screaming and roughhousing. We know the tone of the cries we need to attend to. After being around the bad behaviors so much, we may not even notice them anymore. Then, one day we may find ourselves at a restaurant and all of a sudden, our kids start screaming. Now it's a big deal because we're in public and it's embarrassing. We may become upset with our children but just an hour earlier we had no problem with them acting the same way at home. Bad behavior must be remedied at home, and it is done through consistent discipline.

On a side note, we never counted from one to three for our children to straighten up. As far as we were concerned, we would be teaching our children to disobey an extra three seconds from the time we told them to stop the behavior. I'm not sure where this method originated, but I hear it all the time. We must train our children to be obedient to our voice from the moment they hear it. Why is this important? We are actually training them to be quickly responsive to God's voice. In reality, a three-second delay could mean the difference between life and death. Immediate obedience is best!

When I was younger, my parents used to tell me they were calling the "Little Kid Jailhouse" to come and pick me up. I would beg and cry for them to hang up the phone with a promise to act right. I've heard of parents who told their children they were going to give them away or make them live outside if they didn't start behaving. We should never threaten our children with fear tactics to get them to behave. These are cruel forms of manipulation and although they may be effective for instant behavior modification, they are irresponsible, unloving ways to parent a child.

When disciplining, we should always keep in mind Colossians 3:21 (TLB), "Fathers, don't scold your children so much that they become discouraged and quit trying." I know of a father who was so harsh with his children that once they got out of the house, they turned their backs on their mother and their father, and never set foot in church again. Our wise pastor, John B. Lowe II from Indiana, had a tremendous guideline for parents—rules without relationship breeds rebellion. If our only interaction with our children is enforcing a bunch of do's and don'ts and keeping them on the straight and narrow, we are fostering a potential rebellion. Our aim should be building our children's spirits up, not breaking them down, even in times of discipline. Ephesians 6:4 (NIV) warns, "Fathers, do not provoke your children to anger by the way you treat them. Rather, bring them up with the discipline and instruction that comes from the Lord." Being kind goes a long way with kids. We can still be kind even while disciplining. We should treat them the way we would want to be treated, with respect and dignity (Luke 6:31). The point of discipline is not to make our children feel like losers or unworthy of our love.

Children make childish mistakes because they are CHILDREN. Sometimes they don't have the information they need. For instance, one of my children decided it would be a good idea to put dish soap in the dishwasher since we were out of dishwasher detergent. Of course, half of our kitchen was enveloped in a mountain of suds spilling out of the dishwasher, but how could we be upset? We had never told them not to use the dish soap. This was a childish choice because they just didn't know! Once our children are armed with the right information and our expectations are clearly communicated, we can then say, "We know you'll make a better decision next time."

We need to also be wary of disciplining our toddlers and pre-Ks if we purposefully take them out during their nap time. We should not be upset if our child is cranky or tired because we've stretched them beyond the limits of how they optimally function. Additionally, we need to be mindful of little children's capacity to sit still for long periods of times. If we want to have a conversation with a friend for two hours at a restaurant, it may be best to secure someone to watch our child at home.

As my kids entered the middle school years, I battled with a general distrust of them because of the mistakes I made as a teenager. I was imposing punishment on them for things I had done in the past, without any merit. This breeds contempt in a child. The Lord arrested me before things got out of hand and I allowed myself to believe the best about them. We will cover this topic more in depth in a future chapter. Our job as parents is to come alongside to lovingly guide and correct our children, just like our Heavenly Father does for us.

Disciplining should be a time of teaching not just a time for spanking. Anyone can spank a child long enough and hard enough to stop their actions. We should not be looking for just an instant change in behavior but an understanding of why the actions of our children were wrong, and why God would not want them to do it. This gives us the ability to impart wisdom. We may say, "Wow! Disciplining my child will take work. I'd prefer just to spank them and be done." God's way of disciplining certainly does take work and it is almost NEVER a convenient time to do it the right way.

Kevin and I used our disciplining moments wisely and as our children grew older we needed to spank them less and less. By fifth or sixth grade, we didn't spank them again. Of course, we have had to use other disciplinary methods when needed. We have grounded them some and there have been a few events they didn't get to go to because of it, but not many. If we, as parents, put the time, effort, and consistency in on the front end while our children are small, we will reap great rewards when they are older. Proverbs 29:17 (NKJV) says, "Correct your son, and he will give you rest; Yes, he will give delight to your soul."

Affirmation goes a long way in discipline. When one of our children finally adjusts a bad behavior, instead of silently thinking "It's about time," talk to them about the noticed change. Kevin and I had been consistently working with one of our teenage daughters about not getting upset and remaining calm when we made suggestions on behavior changes. One evening, we brought something to her attention, and instead of flying off the handle, she kept her cool and communicated clearly. I thought, "Praise God! Breakthrough has come!" The next day, I made a point to text her during school to let her know how much I appreciated her response and that it showed she was maturing as a young woman and a Christian. The text back to me was full of heart emojis, thank you's and I love you's!

One of the best ways to show kids how to behave is modeling the behavior for them. When we have a certain persona at home and then reveal a different one at church or in public, kids see the hypocrisy and it is such a turnoff to them. As a past youth leader, I've spoken to many teens who were fed up with their parents' two-faced behavior, and consequently didn't want to have anything to do with God. When I was in high school, it was a regular thing for my parents to ask me to lie to bill collectors on the phone, and to tell those stopping by our business that they weren't there. If we want to spend a fun day with our child and they miss school, we shouldn't tell the teacher that our child was sick so they will not risk having an unexcused absence. If we lie for our children or ask them to lie for us, we shouldn't be surprised when they lie *to* us. "Do as I say and not as I do" is not a good strategy when it comes to parenting. We have a powerful disciplining combination when our words are consistent with our actions.

> *We have all had fathers here on earth who corrected us with discipline. And we respected them. So it is even more important that we accept discipline from the Father of our spirits. If we do this, we will have life. Our fathers on earth disciplined us for a short time in the way they thought was best. But God disciplines us to help us so that we can be holy like him. We don't enjoy discipline when we get it. It is painful. But later, after we have learned our lesson from it, we will enjoy the peace that comes from doing what is right.*
>
> —Hebrews 12:9-11 (ERV)

When our children learn to receive our correction, it will be easier for them to embrace God's correction. We believe godly discipline has been one of the greatest keys in helping shape and mold our arrows into the responsible, respectful, and God-loving young adults they have become. Its importance can never be underestimated or overstated.

## Body Image

It was a sunny and bright Sunday morning and the smell of fresh coffee sifted through the air. We weren't church attenders, so my mom and dad would gather in the living room and pore over every piece of the newspaper. As an eight-year-old girl, this weekly routine was one I looked forward to because my parents were usually in good spirits, well rested, and treated each other kindly. I would always request the "funny papers" or what some would call the comic strips from my dad. I felt like a "big girl" reading my newspaper along with my parents!

This particular day was no different and I excitedly asked my dad for my portion of the paper. He glanced over the top of his newspaper and without warning, and with a disgusted look said, "You are fat!" I stood there stunned trying to grasp what just happened. Did my dad really tell me I am fat? I started sobbing. My mom looked at my dad in horror and said, "Why did you say that?" He said, "She is fat. Just look at her."

Not long afterwards, my mother put me on my first diet. It was Weight Watchers and I had to meticulously follow an eating plan while everyone else in the family got to eat anything they wanted. I particularly remember the ultra-thin slices of bread my mom used to make my sandwiches. Two slices of bread were equal to one regular slice. I felt like an outcast and not worthy of love until I lost the fifteen pounds my parents wanted me to lose. Unfortunately, the eating plan didn't help me.

After my parents divorced, on a summer visit with my dad, my new stepmother thought it would be a good idea to get me some diet pills. I was only eleven years old, but she was doing her best to "help me." When she went to get the diet pills at the salon she normally purchased them from, they were out. Although I didn't get the diet pills, the seed was planted that pills were my answer. As soon as I got home, I found an ad in a magazine for diet pills. I sneaked and stole some money from my mother and ordered the pills. Back in the day, we had to mail our handwritten order and money in an envelope and hope that our products made it back to us in about four to six weeks. My mother intercepted the pills from the mail and brought me straight to her bedroom after I got home from school one day. She asked me about them, and I explained why they were so important to me. She said she didn't feel that they were safe, but she had some vitamin-type diet pills that I could use instead. They were supposedly better than the other diet pills, but they still contained appetite suppressants. They were not a magic pill, though, and the extra weight still lingered.

The summer of my junior year of high school, I was 5' 3" and 135 pounds. This was a good weight zone for me, but I had convinced myself that I was a heavyweight! I buckled down and got down to 108 pounds by basically starving myself. I prided myself on how I could go days at a time without eating, and on the discipline it took to maintain my new ultra skinny body. My parents knew that my weight loss was based on eating very little, but they were happy with my new physique. I clearly remember telling my mother I wasn't going to eat for three days in order to look my best for my senior pictures. She was all for it. Many times, I would almost pass out because I would feel so weak. It was worth it to me, though, for the sake of being thin.

I have had to overcome a lifetime of body image issues that all began as an eight-year-old little girl. What is really upsetting is when I look at the pictures in elementary, middle, and high school—those years I thought I was so fat—I looked like a normal, healthy girl!

Because of my past, protecting my children from negative body image has been a priority. Social media and society bombard them with ideas and standards of what a perfect body looks like. In no way did I want to propagate the unrealistic gauges placed on me as a kid and teenager on being a certain weight or size. I noticed my kids started carrying a little extra weight in the fifth and sixth grade years, and then sprouted up like weeds. I've seen this with other children, too. It must be the body's way of preparing for the growth spurt into puberty. If some parents are not prepared for this, they may bring unnecessary focus on their child's weight while whittling away at their child's self-esteem.

As parents, we should do everything we can to educate our children on good eating and exercise habits. We should exemplify health, rest, and margin in our lives while reinforcing our children's positive self-image. One of my pastors, Keith Cistrunk, wrote a beautiful confession for his young daughter to memorize and say in the mirror each day. It says:

> I am blessed
>
> I am loved
>
> I am fearfully and wonderfully made
>
> I can do all things through Christ which strengthens me.
>
> I shall live and not die and declare the works of the Lord.
>
> God has made me pretty from the inside out.

*For you created my inmost being; you knit me together in my mother's womb. I praise you because I am fearfully and wonderfully made; your works are wonderful, I know that full well. My frame was not hidden from you when I was made in the secret place, when I was woven together in the depths of the earth. Your eyes saw my unformed body; all the days ordained for me were written in your book before one of them came to be. How precious to me are your thoughts, God! How vast is the sum of them!*

—Psalm 139:13-17 (NIV)

When our children understand how valuable and loved they are by their Heavenly Father, it instills a security and confidence that can never be torn away. Sturdy and lasting arrows know they are fearfully and wonderfully created.

## Modesty and Makeup

Our daughters were just eighteen months apart. They were so close in age that I had a blast dressing them up in matching outfits. It was one of my favorite things to do. People used to say, "Do it for as long as you can because there will come a day when they won't want to dress alike." Boy, was that ever true!

As I shopped for their little clothes, I was amazed at how many outfits were adult-like. I wondered, "Why would I want my baby to wear a leopard bikini? Can't they just dress like kids for a while?"

From the time they are infants, society puts the pressure on our children to dress beyond their ages. Our kids, especially our girls, are prime targets in this day and age to grow up way too fast. Girls are beginning to wear makeup earlier and earlier. I've seen them in full foundation, mascara, eyeliner, lipstick—the works in fifth and sixth grades! Many of the social media photo posts, blogs, and videos, glamorize being a sexy, young adult. Embracing childhood is not highly publicized or promoted.

We did our best to help our children be comfortable in whatever season of life they were in. It was okay for them to be kids, and think like kids and dress like kids. When they reached middle school, we talked with our girls about makeup told them it would be best to wait until high school. They had the rest of their lives to wear makeup, so why not hold off and enjoy this time of rocking their beautiful fresh-skinned faces!

As a parent, it's a round-the-clock responsibility to help guide our children on how to dress like young ladies and gentlemen. It's not a natural inclination for them. If we aren't a strong voice, believe me, the roar of social media will happily grab the steering wheel. Acceptable hemlines have been on the rise, literally!  Our guideline for our daughters has always been two to three inches above the knee. Many times they have walked down the stairs to go somewhere only to hear us make any of the following statements: "That's too short. Please, go upstairs and change." "You need to wear leggings with that." "That's too sheer and you'll need to go put on a slip." "That needs an undershirt." "When you sit your skirt rides up too high, so that's not going to work." If it was too tight, too short, too low on top, or it showed too much skin, it wasn't going out the door. Were our daughters always happy with us? Absolutely not! We weren't winning any popularity contests. Our daughters didn't turn out to be prudes. We weren't so restrictive where they couldn't be fashionable or expressive, but we helped them make wise choices when it came to their clothes.

We stressed to our son the importance of good hygiene and putting his best foot forward. We emphasized that EVERYTHING SPEAKS, including appearance. He learned how to represent the Lord in an excellent way and even became skilled in ironing a dress shirt!

Every new style or fad doesn't always have to be a bone of contention. At the time of this writing, ripped jeans are the hottest things since sliced bread. We've reached a compromise with our kids that holes in the knees are acceptable but holes on the upper thigh range or back of thigh are not. I remember traipsing around in sub-zero temperatures with penny loafers and no socks when I was in high school. My parents thought it was the dumbest thing they had ever seen! It was in style and I thought it was cool. Be mindful that some fads don't have to be a make- or-break. We can give our kids the satisfaction of having a few things to look back on and laugh about.

The world will relentlessly endeavor to mold our children into its image. We must be equally vigilant in pointing our children to the Lord and His blueprints for their life.

> *Don't become so well-adjusted to your culture that you fit into it without even thinking. Instead, fix your attention on God. You'll be changed from the inside out. Readily recognize what he wants from you, and quickly respond to it. Unlike the culture around you, always dragging you down to its level of immaturity, God brings the best out of you, develops well-formed maturity in you.*
>
> —Romans 12:2 (MSG)

An arrow can't be mindlessly shaped. With the guidance of the master craftsman they will be formed into His image, inside and out!

# ARROWS MUST BE BALANCED

When an arrow is released from the bow, the push from the back gives the arrow the momentum it needs to fly through the air. The feathers on the end of the arrow give it the spin to keep flying straight and keeps the back of the arrow from raising up and toppling over the front of the arrow. The feathers are crucial in maintaining the arrow's balance to continue to move forward and hit its intended target.

Like the arrow, there are certain things children require to keep them steady and allow them to properly maneuver through life. An unbalanced arrow is ineffective and will always miss the mark. With God's help, our children will be equipped with the balancing spiritual feathers needed to soar towards the bulls-eye.

**The Wisdom of God**

While scarfing down a microwaved honeybun and milk for breakfast, my sister and I excitedly discussed our options for the day. My dad and stepmother had given us the freedom to choose any activity we wanted for that evening. It was our two-week summer vacation at Dad's house. Living so far away from him made our time together a big deal. We were to fl y back to Indiana from Texas after a couple of days, so our choice had to be perfect. Following much deliberation, we decided on miniature golf. Dad wholeheartedly agreed with the idea and promised we would head out after an early evening backyard BBQ.

The anticipation was over the top for this ten-year old girl. I sat on the couch and did my very best to lose myself in the boring television shows as the hours creeped by. I could almost see myself standing on that green Astroturf, hitting one hole-in-one after another.

Later that afternoon, I heard the refrigerator open and I hurried into the kitchen to see my stepmom taking out the hamburger meat to begin making the patties. Finally, we were in meal prep mode which meant I was one step closer to holding that golf club. The phone rang, and my dad picked it up. It was his next-door neighbor who Dad had really taken a liking to since the move to his new house. He and his family had come over almost daily during our vacation. Dad invited them over to eat and within minutes, they arrived with smiles and cases of Coors beer. My first thought was, "Oh no. I hope this doesn't interfere with us going to play miniature golf." My second thought was, "Dad promised we were going so he'll make sure we will."

It wasn't long, and the hamburgers started coming off the grill. I quickly stacked all my fixings together and inhaled my burger within minutes. I tried to make eye contact with my dad, hoping he would get the picture and pick up the pace. Unfortunately, he was engulfed in conversation with his neighbor as they cackled and carried on without any regard for the time or the lack thereof. Their laughter was accompanied by a symphony of clicking tabs and whooshes as they opened beer after beer. I finally got up enough nerve to whisper to my dad "We probably should get going to play miniature golf." He patted me on my shoulder and said, "We'll get going here in just a minute."

The clock kept ticking by when the doorbell rang. It was my dad's father (my "Papa") who dropped by unexpectedly. I was always glad to see Papa, but we had plans and Dad had promised. Papa headed straight to the back porch and was welcomed by bear hugs and cold beers.

I watched the sun drop further and further down the horizon until it was finally dark. It was getting late and if we were going, we would need to go soon. I bravely walked up to my dad and softly said, "Dad, are we still going to play miniature golf?" His muddled answer was slow and slurred. Dad was drunk and now unaware of any plans for miniature golf.

I ran inside the house to the living room couch where I began to cry. I couldn't believe Dad chose to spend this night getting wasted with friends he saw every single day! It was so much more than not being able to play miniature golf with Dad. His choice made me feel rejected, abandoned, undervalued, and unimportant. To top it all off, I was also a little scared seeing my dad in this state of mind.

A few minutes later, Papa, who was pretty intoxicated himself, came and sat beside me. He was surprised to see me crying and asked what was wrong. I explained everything to him and instead of a warm embrace, I received a curt reply, "Oh, quit crying. You'll get drunk one day and do the same thing to your kids!" I yelled out, "No, I won't, Papa. No, I won't!" "Mark my words! You will!" he bantered back as he stumbled towards the patio. Hearing the screen door close behind him, I shouted deep inside myself, "I won't!" while making a sacred vow to my future children.

I am sure my dad and Papa never would have guessed that their actions on that summer night would have made such an impact on my life. They both passed away many years ago, but I know if they were alive today, and they heard this story, they would have been deeply sorry. It just goes to show how our choices and words can have a lasting effect on our children and grandchildren.

I know Dad and Papa were only operating in the knowledge they had at the time. Thankfully, God's wisdom far surpasses our limited human knowledge.

James 1:5 (NIV) says, "If any of you lacks wisdom, you should ask God, who gives generously to all without finding fault, and it will be given to you." All we have to do is ask God and He will give us the abundance of wisdom needed to parent our children. I know this sounds funny, but God's wisdom showed me ways to parent by doing the opposite of some of the things my parents did! Wisdom revealed how to love when it would have been easy to hate. Wisdom demonstrated how to speak kindly when I wanted to verbally tear my kids to shreds. Wisdom exhibited promoting peace when I could have infused pure chaos into the atmosphere. Wisdom helped me to make BETTER choices based on my past experiences.

As much as we try to be good parents and be led by the wisdom of God, we never get it right one hundred percent of the time. That doesn't mean we purposefully mess up, but God's wisdom will teach our children to learn from our mistakes. When we fumble, we should be quick to tell our children, "I didn't do that right and I'm sorry. I am actively doing my best to change this. I hope that you'll see how this does not promote peace in our home or bring about success." We can be assured that God will show our children through His wisdom how to be better parents, better spouses, better employees, and better friends.

The wisdom of God will also insulate our children from things the enemy would like to use to destroy them. Psalm 121:7 (NKJV) says, "The LORD shall preserve you from all evil; He shall preserve your soul." I once heard someone say that our children are like canned peaches in a mason jar. They may be looking through the glass, but what's on the outside of the jar won't get to them on the inside. Although they may unintentionally witness evil things, whether at school or with other kids, God will preserve them from the destructive impact those things could possibly make on their life.

Arrows need a steadier that allows them to stream smoothly through the air. The wisdom of God supplies the important balance and perspective needed for children to thrust towards their God-given destiny.

## Gifts

When my niece, Gloria, was about four years old, my brother-in-law and sister-in-law signed her up for dance lessons. She was a real ham and a born superstar with a definite flair for dancing. Although my niece was little, the expenses for the lessons, the tap and ballet shoes, and the fancy costumes were not. After six months of rehearsing, the long anticipated dance recital was finally here. The auditorium was packed with grandmas, grandpas, aunts, uncles, and of course, the beaming parents with their video equipment and cameras in hand. Act after act, I witnessed many jubilant and extremely talented children performing like celebrities as they danced their hearts out. My niece's troupe pranced with confidence as they entered the stage and waited to hear the first magic note of their dance number. After a few seconds of awkward silence, our attention was directed to the side of the stage beside the curtain. It was a mother doing all she could to coax her little girl out on stage with the other mini-ballerinas. Her daughter clung to her like she was about to fall off the edge of the Grand Canyon.

With a look of sheer horror, the little girl began to sob and with one scoop, her mother picked her up and exited the stage. I knew this mother from church and was able to talk to her after the recital. She was disappointed that her daughter would not go through with the dance. I agreed that it was unfortunate with all of the work and expense invested in the lessons and costumes. The mother confided that her daughter really didn't seem to like dancing but that in time, she knew she would grow to love it just like she did as a kid. This mom didn't understand what was blatantly obvious to everyone else—her daughter did not want to be a dancer and it didn't matter how many cute tutus or glitter body suits she wore, they weren't going to make her one.

God is the giver of children's gifts and abilities. Parents have a responsibility to recognize those gifts and then facilitate opportunities for those gifts to grow. Kevin and I didn't buy into the pressure of putting our children in sports or piano lessons at three years old. We waited to see what type of personalities they took on and what things they were interested in. We didn't throw money into the wind trying to force our children to do something we thought they would like. It wasn't a popular choice as we watched many of our peers taking their young kids to and from multiple practices and events.

Austin played some sports in elementary and middle school, but they were never his thing. We had to be okay with letting go of the all-American dream of a quarterback son or basketball star. He took a particular interest in freestyle biking in middle school, and he excelled in the sport. He saved and paid for his own custom bike which he painstakingly fashioned together like an artist designing a masterpiece. It kept him fit and busy during his high school years and continues to be an enjoyable hobby in college. It was a God-ordered step which afforded him many opportunities to witness the love of Christ to other freestyle bikers. Additionally, his knack for taking things apart and putting them back together led him down the path of mechanical engineering. He has never doubted this career choice and believes God has called him to design world changing inventions.

When our children share with us something they would like to do for a career that we don't agree with, we should not act shocked or cut them down right away. For example, Kamryn, was all about going to New York and being on Broadway when she was in middle school. We knew she really loved theatre and although we sensed in our hearts that she would most likely go another direction as she got older, we didn't cut her down and say, "Kam, that's not going to happen." We actually helped her get into an outside theatre group and she honed her skills. As she was nearing her junior year in high school, her direction changed and she felt a call to children's ministry. We allowed God to do a work in her heart and speak clearly to her in His own time. All of her investment in theatre was not wasted because it definitely boosted her confidence and her ability to speak in public—those things will help her tremendously in ministry!

If our children are good at a lot of things, it doesn't mean they should be doing them all. For example, Kamryn has a beautiful singing voice. She had the privilege of being asked to sing on our worship team at church. She was also very involved as a pre-K teacher on Sundays. Usually there was a scheduling conflict between her teaching and worship team schedules on the weekends. She realized after a few weeks that although she enjoyed serving in both areas, she would need to choose one of those ministries where she would be most effective. Because Kamryn felt a strong pull to become a children's pastor one day, she laid down serving on the worship team to give her full attention and energy to the pre-K class. It is tempting to jam pack our children's schedules with personal activities, especially if there are a lot of opportunities for them to serve and participate on great teams. However, they will benefit more from doing one or two things with full force and passion than ten things with mediocrity. In high school, there is pressure to fill up college resumes with clubs, titles, and accolades but from experience, colleges put more merit into a few purposeful and productive things than a whole list of meaningless titles and club participations.

Proverbs 22:6 (AMPC) says, "Train up a child in the way he should go [and in keeping with his individual gift or bent], and when he is old he will not depart from it." Many interpret this verse in relationship to their children's spiritual training. The main focus is actually acknowledging and cultivating our children's God-given purpose and being sensitive to how they are uniquely designed. One of the worst statements we can tell our children is, "You can be anything you want to be," and present life like a smorgasbord of dreams for the taking. The better statement would be, "You can be anything God has called you to be." If we diligently direct our children according to their gifts, when they are old they will still be flourishing in their purpose. Another wonderful scripture to back this up is 2 Peter 1:10 (GNT), "So then, my friends, try even harder to make God's call and his choice of you a permanent experience; if you do so, you will never abandon your faith."

It saddens me to see young adults aimlessly hopping from job to job without any direction. It screams to me somewhere down the line that a parent has either missed or ignored signals of what their child likes or is gifted to do. Sometimes the issue may be the child knows what they want to do, but the parents are not in agreement because the career wouldn't yield the money or success they think their child should have. The child then floats around for years trying to make something work but never comes to a place of purpose. We must be very cautious on how we influence our children concerning their calling. Be mindful that they will never be fully satisfied in life unless they are doing what they were created to do. Using how much money they will or won't make as a decision-making filter is wrong. Also, if they need certain educational requirements to fulfill their calling, don't steer them in a different direction because of the expense of gaining a degree or certification. I have seen many young adults stalled in a holding pattern due to educational financial fears. I believe when children obey the leading of the Lord concerning their purpose, great blessing and provision will follow them, not just financially but also physically, relationally, and emotionally. Where God guides, He will provide!

It is important to make allowances for children to dream about their God-given direction. Austin was set on a certain college that we were open to him attending. During college preview visits to this school and some others, he realized it was not the best fit for him. Proverbs 16:9 (NIV) says, "We can make our plans, but the **LORD** determines our steps." By giving him the freedom to move forward with the college he thought would be his choice, he was directed to another college that was better suited for him. God will also order our children's steps to the right people at the right time. Proverbs 18:16 (NKJV) says, "A man's gift makes room for him and brings him before great men." Although gift in this verse is speaking primarily about a physical gift, I believe a man's God-given purpose and gifting can also pave the way to divine opportunities and connections.

One of the best prayers Kevin and I have found to pray for our children concerning their purpose is in Ephesians 1:17-19 (NLT):

> *Dear God, I ask that you give our children spiritual wisdom and insight, so they might grow in their knowledge of You. I pray that their hearts will be flooded with light so that they can understand the confident hope You have called them to. May they grasp the inheritance you have given them in the saints and realize the exceeding greatness of Your power in their lives. In Jesus name. Amen.*

Dorothy in the Wizard of Oz realized in the end that the ruby slippers on her feet always held the power to get her home but she never knew it. What should be obvious is sometimes blocked from our view. Asking God to open our children's spiritual eyes and shed the light of His truth, will bring the clarity and confidence needed to achieve all He's called them to be.

It is of utmost importance for children to know and recognize their high calling in Christ Jesus. As they operate in their gifts, just like the feathers on the arrow, they will have the stability to maintain the intended flight trajectory towards success.

## Identity

"Remember who you are!" Mufasa declared to his son, Simba. In one of my favorite scenes from the movie *The Lion King*, Simba's father gives his son a sharp wakeup call to his identity. It is our responsibility as parents to promote and protect our children's identity, but we need to be keenly aware of what that is. Perhaps your son is an excellent baseball player, has invested a great deal of time practicing and competing, and has his sights set on playing in the big leagues. For him—who has breathed, eaten, and slept baseball since his childhood—it would be quite tempting to be defined as a baseball player. A scholastic high achiever may view themselves as an academic scholar as they immerse themselves in studying and earning straight A's to get that full ride to college. Based on the accomplishments of their family, whether in business, ministry, or military service, some children's identities are wrapped up in legacy and the family name.

What happens if our baseball player receives a career-ending injury? What happens if our academic scholar gets a bad grade or doesn't get the full-ride scholarship? What happens if our child somehow dishonors the family name? If their identities are based on their performance, they will view themselves as failures. The pseudo identity they have formed will pressure them into focusing on what they have done and not on who they really are.

In the previous section, we learned about the importance of children operating in their gifts and callings. Lines can easily be blurred between children excelling in their gifts and talents, and the source of their true identity.

So, what is their true identity? Galatians 2:20 (ERV) says, "I am not the one living now—it is Christ living in me. I still live in my body, but I live by faith in the Son of God. He is the one who loved me and gave himself to save me."

Once children declare Jesus as their Lord and Savior, their identity stems from Jesus living through them. Just as Mufasa admonished his son, we should exhort our children to "remember who they are," not in themselves but who they are in Christ. May they daily walk in the security of knowing how deeply loved and valued they are by God. May they not rely on their own efforts to bring them to a place of value and self-worth. May they realize it's in Christ they live and move and have their being (Acts 17:28). May they see that God does not measure them by what they do but by what Jesus has done for them.

Christ's love is the ground in which children can sink their roots (Ephesians 3:17). It also provides the foundation for them to confidently stand in the One who gave His life for them. When our arrows embrace their true identity in Jesus, it provides the proper balancing mechanism and focus to ensure their mission stays on course.

## Family Devotions

When my children were little, I envisioned the day when they would all file into the living room with their Bibles under their arms with big smiles on their faces ready for our family devotion time. Of course, our goal would be to have devotions every night before bed. How difficult could that be? As life progressed, we soon realized that our goals were a bit too lofty to achieve. We have had planned and structured devotions, but most of our focused time on God's Word has happened organically.

> *These words which I command you today shall be in your heart. You shall teach them diligently to your children, and shall talk of them when you sit in your house, when you walk by the way, when you lie down, and when you rise up. You shall bind them as a sign on your hand, and they shall be as frontlets between your eyes. You shall write them on the doorposts of your house and on your gates.*
>
> —Deuteronomy 6:6-9 (NKJV)

This verse encourages us to maximize every moment we can to teach our children God's Word and show them how to apply that instruction in real-life situations. Every day provides multiple chances to teach our children in the ways of the Lord.

Isaiah 28:9-10 (NKJV) says, "Whom will he teach knowledge? And whom will he make to understand the message? Those just weaned from milk? Those just drawn from the breasts? For precept must be upon precept, precept upon precept, line upon line, here a little, there a little." The prophets and ministers of old taught the knowledge of God and His will in small, repetitious doses of truth that could be easily absorbed and understood by the hearer. The Holy Spirit will help us build our children's spiritual foundation exactly the same way. Bit by bit, story by story, scripture by scripture, God's truth will edge its way into their hearts.

We can make a point to weave the Word of God into our family's daily conversations and interactions. We should be sensitive to spiritual download opportunities and seize the treasured teaching moments the Lord gives us.

One idea for devotion time with small children is to choose one short verse to focus on the entire week. For example, Ephesians 6:10 says, "I am strong in the Lord and the power of His might." The first day we may talk about the difference of being strong physically and strong spiritually. The second day we could discuss what Jesus did so we could be strong. The third day we could give an example from the Bible about someone who walked in the strength of the Lord or maybe give them our own testimony. The fourth day we could have them draw an example of what this verse means to them. The fifth day we may teach them a chorus to a song that reinforces their strength in God. All the while, our children are memorizing this verse and receiving more clarity and revelation on walking in God's power and might.

Another great option for elementary age and up, is to have a weekly or bi-weekly devotional and assign one member of the family to share a five- to ten-minute teaching on any biblical subject they choose. Preparing for the devotional helps our children break down God's Word for themselves and gives them practice verbalizing what's in their hearts. Fast forward several years, Kevin and I have witnessed the impact these devotion times have made upon our children as they are now being called upon to teach God's Word in youth group, pre-K classes and our fifth/sixth grade group. They are comfortable sharing their faith and testimonies because we lovingly placed a demand on them to do so at home in a safe and nonjudgmental atmosphere.

Guiding our children to have their own personal time with God is one of the most important things we can do as a parent.

I highly recommend the children's devotionals found at Kenneth Copeland Ministries. My children frequently use the "Load Up" devotional found on their website at kcm.org. The teachings are short and powerful, and they end with a confessional prayer. It is such a joy seeing our children's Bible's highlighted and underlined as they dive deep into exploring God's Word.

Without the grounding effects of family and personal devotions, our arrows would spin wildly out of control. The Word of God offers them the depth and security to steer with confident direction.

**Bible Reading, Prayer, and Worship**

Dorothy Law Nolt wrote a poem called "Children Learn What They Live." Just the title of this poem alone is a rich truth. The habits and values our children embrace stem from what they live out on a daily basis. What our children see us do makes all the difference in the world! My pastor has made the statement many times, "Preach the gospel, and if necessary, use words." We can talk to our children until we're blue in the face about what they should be doing and how they should be acting. The best way to get our point across is to mirror the actions and attitudes we are asking from them.

When it comes to spiritual things, most will be caught and not taught. Kevin and I have always had a deep desire to see our children walk with the Lord and have a close personal relationship with Him. We have never hidden our relationship with God from our children. They have seen Kevin and me reading our Bible many times. It should never be a weird occurrence for our children to see us crack open our Bible. If Bible reading is not yet a part of your daily routine, why not start today? A multitude of Bible reading plans are available at www.bible.com to help us make God's Word a regular part of our day. Colossians 3:16 (NKJV) says, "Let the word of Christ dwell in you richly in all wisdom, teaching and admonishing one another in psalms and hymns and spiritual songs, singing with grace in your hearts to the Lord." We must let the word of Christ dwell in us. Once we make the choice to allow God's Word entry into our hearts, we'll be equipped with the wisdom and ability to teach and admonish our children.

As we read the Bible, we should get a notebook and write out scriptures that are particularly meaningful. We can then share our observations with our children and ask them what they think about a particular Bible passage—what does it mean to them? If they are encountering a life challenge, we can show them what God's Word has to say about their situation. If we don't know, a quick Google search for scriptures relating to a particular topic is an excellent way to go. Another great little book is called *God's Promises for Your Every Need* written by Dr. A.L. Gill. This book is broken down in categories of life's challenges with applicable scriptures for each topic. Little children are very receptive to God's Word and their tender hearts are ready to believe the promises of God. We can share a simplistic thought or scripture with them, and may be surprised how much they have to say! We can encourage our children with the Word of God. Let them hear us proclaiming God's promises over the entire family. They will soon learn that for every problem, God has a solution in His Word.

Since children learn by example, hearing us pray is very important. Prayer is simply having a conversation with God. Just like any conversation we would have, it will vary in length, subject, and intensity. Philippians 4:6-7 (CEV) says, "Don't worry about anything, but pray about everything. With thankful hearts offer up your prayers and requests to God." How many times a day does life bring something to worry about? I know I have multiple opportunities to worry in a day, but it isn't God's desire that we stress and strain over troubles that come our way. His best is that we not worry about anything. Yes, it says that— ANYTHING! What are we supposed to do instead? Pray about EVERYTHING!

We can also ask the Lord to help us be sensitive to seize moments of prayer with our children. Nothing is too small to bring to God in prayer. I remember a time when DeLaney was about eight years old. I was driving with her and her friend and we passed a Chick-Fil-A in a neighboring town. The girls began to talk about how delicious the chicken was and what a pain it was to drive so far to go the restaurant. I said, "You know what girls? We can ask God for a Chick-Fil-A in our neighborhood." They looked at me strangely and I said, "He cares about everything we care about. If you want a Chick-Fil-A closer, then He can make that happen." We immediately asked God for the right location, the right people, and the provision needed to build a Chick-Fil-A close to us. I told the girls to always remember this prayer because it wouldn't be long, and we would have our Chick-Fil-A. Do you know it wasn't a year and a half later and we got our Chick-Fil-A! Not only did we get one ChickFil-A at the front of our town, we got a second one that was very close to our house. Will those girls remember how God brought a Chick-Fil-A to their town? They sure will! They have proof positive that God hears them and answers their prayers.

As parents, we should be quick to pray with our family. As situations arise, we can bring them to God. We should make it a habit to talk to Him throughout the day. When our children shared something with us that they needed direction on, many times Kevin and I would say, "Let's pray about that right now." We can show our children that prayer is a way of life and not just something to be done on Sundays at church.

We lived in the Pittsburgh, Pennsylvania area when our children were little. Fall is one of my favorite seasons and the gorgeous hues of gold, pink, and burgundy foliage there are absolutely breathtaking. One morning drive led me and the kids down a winding road wedged between two hills arrayed with beautifully colored trees. I instantly pointed out the grandeur of what we were seeing and said, "Let's all thank God for the pretty trees He made." From the back of the mini-van I heard three sweet, high-pitched voices proclaiming "thank you" to the Creator of the Universe. Whether it was white puffy clouds, brilliant sunsets, or glorious rainbows, Kevin and I were purposeful in showing our children how and why to praise God in those simple moments. Our twenty-one year old son recently posted a picture of a lovely sunrise bouncing off the skies on his Instagram account with the post "Wow God! You are amazing!" I couldn't help but smile.

Living a life of thanksgiving before our children will help prevent self-centeredness and arrogance in their lives. Being thankful will shift their perspective and help them see the good in their world. Our pastor, Brett Jones, says, "It's hard to offend a grateful person." That is some truth right there! A thankful heart yields great dividends.

Choosing to live our spiritual lives in plain view of our children can prevent or break down any barriers the devil would like to build in them. Our children's trust in God will deepen as they witness His faithfulness at work in us. Like the proven balancing feathers on the arrow, their observations of us living wholeheartedly for God will bolster their ability to reach places beyond their highest hopes and dreams.

## Spending Time with Your Children

Kevin and I had the privilege of having John B. and Debbie Lowe II from Warsaw, Indiana, as our spiritual mentors and pastors when we were first married. We were young at twenty-three and twenty years old, and had a lot to learn. Pastor Lowe and Pastor Debbie taught us how to grow in our marriage and gave us important insight on being future parents. One thing we have never forgotten is how Pastor Lowe spelled the word love —T.I.M.E. Sharing our time with someone is one of the greatest acts of love we can give.

Time was easy to give when my children were younger. I was blessed to be able to stay at home with them until my last child was in kindergarten. They needed a lot of care, guidance, and attention, and were usually thrilled to spend time with me. Something happened in middle school and the early years of high school, though. I noticed—especially with my daughters—a natural inclination to pull away from us. Maybe it was hormonal, as there is a bridge to cross between being a kid and growing into a young adult. It's a difficult thing to have to navigate for a parent. In this season of life, we must be more proactive to push in and have conversations with our kids. To prevent losing touch with who they are, we can't allow too much distance to come between us and our children. It may be tempting to relax during this time and basically let them raise themselves. Our children still need us and our guidance, but in a different way. It is also important that they know we care and are a strong support in their life.

I have noticed two particular times that usually foster meaningful and rich conversations with pre-teens and teenage children. The first one is driving together in the car. The avoidance of eye contact is very non-threatening, relieves pressure, and allows for more transparency and openness. It's a much better way to talk than sitting directly across from each other at a table. We should never underestimate the simple drive to the grocery store, or the trip home from soccer practice.

The other time we must be ready for kids to talk, especially teenagers, is when we are about to go to bed. For whatever reason, this is the hour they really open up. Frequently, I've been seconds away from turning my bed lamp off to go to sleep and one (or all) of my children mosey in and plop on my bed. All it takes is one or two questions, and the floodgates open. When they were infants, we were more than willing to sacrifice sleep. Just because they are older, we have to be willing to seize those precious moments and not say, "I'm tired. Get out of here."

As our children confide in us, listen intently. We should never act shocked at what they have to say. Remain calm or they will clam up very quickly!

Children love bedtime rituals, and this can be an extra special time to prepare them for a peaceful and restful night's sleep, and make lasting memories. When I was a small child, my mother would oftentimes trace her fingers over my eyebrows, my closed eyes, my nose, around my mouth and circle my entire face from forehead to chin. It was one of my favorite moments with her. I carried on this tradition at bedtime with my children and they still talk about it with great pleasure. Just between us, I've even gotten a few face-trace requests from them as teenagers. A special prayer time, reading a short book or nose kisses at bedtime are simple but impactful times we can share with our children. Kevin and I always did our best, even when they were older, to kiss them good night even if they were asleep. We realized there would come a day—sooner than we would realize—they would be grown, and those night-time kisses would be a thing of the past.

We should take time to laugh every day with our kids. Life can get serious, but joy is essential. Nehemiah 8:10 (NIV) says, "The joy of the Lord is your strength." Take a breather and look for the funny side of life. Kevin and I have laughed through a lot of hard times, and we always came out victoriously on the other side! We can teach our kids that a merry heart really does do good like a medicine (Proverbs 17:22, NIV). Our kids can vouch that times of hearty laughter together abound in the Schafer home.

Life gets busy, but we should make a point to tell our children that we love them every day. I've mentioned it before but in the teen years our kids aren't usually as verbal, so it is easy to not talk to them as much. Although our words may be fewer, we shouldn't skimp on saying, "I love you." We should text them, write on a sticky note and put it on the bathroom mirror, and take advantage of opportunities to look them straight in the eye and tell them those three beautiful, encouraging words. We should take the time to say it. Remember, love never fails (1 Corinthians 13:8, NIV).

When children are little, hugs are plenteous and frequent. During the teenage years, hugging almost becomes foreign and taboo. Although they may not seem like they welcome our big ol' hug, they really do. We must take time to hug our children every day. My pastor, Brett Jones, says it is vitally important that girls need to know how to be hugged in a non-sexual way. Dads, don't be afraid to hug and kiss your girls even into their teenage years. Don't leave them starving for the touch of a man. Your hug will relay a strong message of security and the real love of a father.

Dads, please don't leave all of the responsibility on the mother to entertain your daughter. Kevin will often take one or both of our daughters on an impromptu ride to Starbucks, or a walk around the block, or to the grocery store to pick out some cookie dough to bake. Planned daddy dates are great. Do them when you can, but never discount unplanned God-given moments to spend time with your daughter. Time at home is wonderful, but teenage girls especially LOVE to get out and about on the town. Make an effort! Also, remember to not squelch your children's spontaneity. It's a gift! Some things are just fun for them and may not be fun for you. Never make your time with them seem like an inconvenience. Little moments here and there add up—you are strengthening your relationship as a strong and supportive dad.

One of my favorite books on child-raising is *Bringing Up Boys* by Dr. James Dobson. I believe everyone who is raising a son should read this book for amazing insight on how a boy grows into a man. One of the key points that stuck out to me is that around the age of three to five years old, a boy naturally starts to gravitate towards his father in order to form his masculine identity. It can be quite startling to a mother when her son, who normally wants his "Mommy," starts wanting his "Daddy." As moms we need to recognize this transition and not interfere with what God is doing during this time. Kevin confidently took the reins and brought Austin under his wing. Austin helped his dad hold tools as he fixed cars, worked on multiple projects together, and shared valuable time together throughout the years. Austin learned what it meant to be a God-fearing man full of integrity and excellent character because of the purposeful relationship Kevin had with him. The things Kevin taught him were not a natural inclination for me as a woman. For instance, we had recently moved to Texas, and for the first time we lived in a neighborhood where kids were able to ride their bikes on the street. Austin was in sixth grade and he asked if he could ride his bike around the neighborhood. My first response was "absolutely not." I was thinking about safety, so I thought I was being a responsible parent. Kevin intervened and said, "Keeley, we are going to let him ride his bike. Nothing is going to happen to him. He is a responsible kid and he will be fine." It was a hard moment, but I watched from a distance as Austin's bike turned around the corner of the block. Little did I realize this was a certain rite of passage for a boy that had to be done. I am thankful for Kevin's leadership, and we surely have an awesome son to prove it, as well as two incredible daughters!

Sadly, I realize there are times when a father is either totally out of the picture, or doesn't take his role as father as seriously as he should. Psalm 23:1 (NIV) says, "The Lord is my Shepherd, I lack nothing." I truly believe that God will fill any gaps in our child's life through mentorships and strong men to help them guide the way. Be sensitive to the Lord, and He will bring about the connections needed for our children to flourish and grow into the young men and women He has called them to be.

When we do take time with our children to do something extra special, we need to be cautious of something. Let's say we take our kids to Disneyworld, or to a pricey concert of their favorite artist, or anywhere that will utilize more cash than we normally spend. The last thing we want to do is make them feel guilty for being there. This may sound absurd, but it can happen. Throwing out phrases such as the following deeply diminish the special experience for your children: "I hope you appreciate all of the things we're doing for you right now." "Lots of kids don't get to do this." "Do you know how much money we're spending for you to do this?" "You'd better be thankful." "I don't think you are acting grateful enough for this trip."

> *Do not eat the bread of a selfish man, or desire his delicacies;*
> *For as he thinks in his heart, so is he [in behavior—one who*
> *manipulates]. He says to you, "Eat and drink," Yet his heart*
> *is not with you [but it is begrudging the cost].*
>
> —Proverbs 23:6-7 (AMPC)

This man's irritation about the price tag of the meal he provided prevented him from experiencing the joyful fellowship and memories the meal could have afforded. While stingily eating the food with his guests, he missed the gift of the moment. With this in mind, instead of saying to our children, "Do you know how much money we're spending on you?" how about saying, "We are happily investing in you." Instead of saying, "We hope you are thankful for what we are doing," we could say, "We are so thankful to be able to do this for you." Instead of saying, "Lots of kids don't get to do this," try saying, "God has blessed us, and He cares about you so much that He has made a way for us to do this." Instead of saying, "We can't wait to get home because this trip is costing us a fortune," a great option would be, "We're so thankful we get to share this trip together. It's a memory we'll always cherish with you."

Purposeful, heartfelt time spent with our children is never wasted time. It is a building block God uses to strengthen our relationships. It's a vehicle to impart valuable wisdom and make memories for a lifetime. Without the gift of time, our arrows would be subjected to a lopsided flight full of zigs and zags. If we want to make sure to provide the stability they need to be laser focused, layers upon layers of time investments are the key to driving our arrows home.

## The Church and Youth Group

It was the first Sunday of January 1986. Mom said it was a new year and time for a fresh start spiritually. We had never gone to church consistently as a family so this was a big deal. I was sixteen and a junior in high school, and my three other sisters were thirteen, four, and one. My baby brother was only a few weeks old. The house was bustling with activity as we hurriedly readied ourselves to get to church on time. New Life Christian Church and World Outreach was only a few years old and was holding their meetings in an elementary school gym. I remember walking in together, like we were on a mission. I couldn't put my finger on it exactly, but it seemed the importance of this moment was very significant. The small band began to play and even though the choruses were simple, they contained a tangible power and awesome reverence for God that captured my attention. Debbie Lowe, the pastor's wife, led worship and not only was she beautiful, she had a glow about her as she sang with unhindered focus on Jesus. Pastor Lowe preached a relevant and fiery message that contained truths from God's Word that I had never heard before. We left the church that day exhilarated and a bit curious to hear more.

After arriving home, we began to compare notes and came to the consensus that we would like to revisit the church. "They do have a service on Sunday nights at six p.m. We could go to the service this evening," my mom informed.

Now don't get me wrong, I really enjoyed the service, but I definitely didn't want to be one of those fanatical Christians who went to church every time the doors were open. I murmured something to my mom like, "I have homework, we'll get home too late, etc." Whatever it was, my mom agreed and said it was probably best not to go. As soon as she turned around to walk away, I looked at my thirteen-year-old sister, Sheila, shot my arms up in the air, and whispered, "Yes!" Sheila immediately yelled, "Mom! Keeley is celebrating that we're not going tonight!" Mom spun back around and said, "Oh, she is? Well, it looks like we're going then!"

Little did I know my mother's firm decision would change the direction of my life forever. I don't recall ever missing a service after that day, and not going to church was definitely not up for discussion with my mom. Within a couple of months, I had radically given my heart to Christ and never looked back. Pastor Lowe and Debbie became important mentors and the church became a place for me to grow spiritually and develop as a leader. Attending this church was also a catalyst for me going to Oral Roberts University in Tulsa, Oklahoma. I ended up meeting the love of my life, Kevin, there and the rest is history.

I have received several frantic phone calls from parents asking for emergency counseling for their rebellious teenagers through the

Member Care department at the church where I serve. I will usually ask if their child has been active in our student ministry groups and/or regularly attending church. Sadly, the majority of the time the answer is "no." Some excuses are, "They don't really like to come to youth group." "They are not comfortable being around new people." "My work schedule doesn't allow me to bring them regularly." "We've got a lot going on. We come to church off and on." "They play sports, so we can't come." In a nutshell, their hopes were for us to meet with their teenager, cure them in a couple of hours, and go back to life as usual.

My church in Houston recently constructed a new worship center and administrative building. I remember my excitement as the bulldozers and other heavy equipment showed up onsite. "It's just a matter of time now, and we'll have our new building," I thought. Little did I know that months would drone on where the property looked basically unchanged. I saw all the people and heavy equipment moving around from day to day, but I didn't see a wall or anything going up. I asked our building manager what was happening, and he said it takes a long time to build a solid foundation for a building of this scale. Just like our church building project, our children's spiritual lives take substantial time to develop. Lasting foundations take constant and earnest effort. It's a lengthy process that may seem mundane and less than spectacular; however, it is vital to the success and longevity of the structure. Cutting corners in the foundation is risky business and is just asking for trouble. Thus, cutting out a vital part of spiritual development for our children in church attendance and becoming active participants in the youth group is opening a door to potential problems.

I always say "the best form of counseling is regular church attendance." Our church leadership prays and seeks the Lord on the messages for the congregation. How many times have we walked out of a service thinking, "That was just what I needed to hear today"? It wasn't just luck but the Holy Spirit speaking through the minister. Those messages build on top of each other and help us form a foundation for living. It's not possible for a youth leader or pastor to cram a year's worth of teaching into an hour of counseling with our children. As parents, it's our responsibility to ensure our children are taking full advantage of the spiritual development opportunities available, including church and youth group attendance. Church youth camps and retreats are also vitally important as they allow our children the liberty to give complete focus, usually without strict time restraints, on God's presence. I know—for myself and for my children—those moments birthed valuable insights and direction for our futures.

I wonder how my life would have ended up if my mother had not been adamant that we would go to church and not just be spectators but contributors. As parents, we should not give our children the option to attend church or youth group. Kevin and I would not give our kids a "pass" to miss church if they attended a sleepover on Saturday night. They would take their church clothes to the sleepover and we would pick them up on our way to church, because they understood it was a priority for our family. If a child does not want to eat vegetables, a responsible parent will make sure they eat a balanced meal, even against their child's fits of disgust. The child doesn't see the importance of that meal and how eventually it will cause them to grow and develop into strong and healthy adults. Consistent spiritual meals at home and at church, cause our children to develop into spiritually mature believers.

Whether it is a sport or extracurricular activity or whatever excuse is taking our children away from church, count the cost. It's not worth it!

Splitting our attendance between churches or youth groups only brings confusion. Committing to membership at one church as a family, allows our roots to grow deep in relationships, service, and spiritual maturity. Psalm 92:13 (NKJV) says, "Those who are planted in the house of the LORD shall flourish in the courts of our God." Just as it is impossible for a plant to grow in two different pots, so it is with trying to commit to several churches at once. If any of our children attend a youth group outside of the family's church, we should seek the Lord to see where the entire family should attend. This will bring spiritual stability and focus to the family as we flourish together in the house of the Lord.

Kevin and I never made our children lift their hands or praise the Lord during worship if they were sitting with us in service. We wanted those actions to be a heart choice and not a rehearsed habit or ritual. However, we always expected them to honor the Word of God and His presence at all times. Luke 8:18 (NIV) says, "Therefore consider carefully how you listen." We asked them to listen with their full attention. They were not allowed to sleep during the service or play on their phones. Our church normally had age-appropriate services during church up to about middle school. Most of the time our children were attending those services. I have witnessed many well-meaning parents bringing their babies into the sanctuary to "get them used to being in the service," or for whatever reason they didn't want them to go to the nursery. Although some babies do well, many do not in this environment.

When babies are born, they have two innate fears. One is the fear of falling and the other one is the fear of loud noises. Imagine a preacher hitting home his message with moments of extreme volume and emphasis right in the microphone. To a small child, it sounds like someone is yelling at them. Bottom line, it's a scary sound. No wonder these poor little darlings are screaming. Believe me, they will enjoy the nursery so much better and we will get to enjoy the service. If they are keeping quiet, it may be because they are getting an unlimited supply of Cheerios from mom or dad so there are no outbursts. Unfortunately, mom or dad are so focused on keeping their child quiet, they aren't able to concentrate on what the minister is saying. Usually our babies, toddlers, and pre-K children's capacities are exhausted by expecting them to sit still and be quiet for about an hour and a half in service. It's a blessing to have age-appropriate classes for our children during service, so we should take full advantage of them.

Our children have always had a love for God's house and his people. Some have made comments to us that it is amazing that not one of them had a negative attitude toward coming to church or serving the Lord. Of course, prayer and God's faithfulness has been key to their success, but I also believe Kevin and I have been examples to our children, showing them church is an extension of our love for the Lord. Gathering together is an important part of refueling and training to go into the world and preach the Gospel to every creature. It sends mixed messages about our commitment when we drop our youth off at the door to go to their service, and head to the restaurant while the adult service is going on in the sanctuary. It confuses our children when we show that we don't need to hear the Word of God, but they do.

If we want our children to make the Lord a priority, then He must be ours. I think of the story in Acts 16 of the jailer who asked Paul and Silas what he needed to do to be saved. They told him to believe in the Lord Jesus Christ and he and his WHOLE HOUSEHOLD would be saved. This man took the lead spiritually, fully committed his life to Christ, and his household followed him with that decision.

> *This is not the time to pull away and neglect meeting together, as some have formed the habit of doing, because we need each other! In fact, we should come together even more frequently, eager to encourage and urge each other onward as we anticipate that day dawning.*
>
> —Hebrews 10:25 (TPT)

God values corporate worship because he knows the power it contributes to our daily walk with him. Regular church attendance empowers our arrows to steadily soar on track, even in the most adverse conditions.

## Don't Feed Fears

I need a pastor to come to our house as soon as possible," the nervous woman exclaimed. From the moment I answered the phone in our Member Care office, I could tell this woman was extremely upset. "What exactly is happening?" I asked as I tried to gather the details. "Our window blinds are going up and down on their own and some of our doors are opening and closing by themselves. My kids and I are getting scared and we need someone to come and pray for us and our home," she explained.

We coordinated a visit a few days later with one of our pastors and a trusted member of our church. As they entered the house, the mother and her two older teenage sons reiterated what they had been experiencing. Our wise pastor explained that they held the ultimate authority in their home and he instructed them on how to pray and anoint their home with oil. As they made their way praying throughout the house, they arrived in the game room area. Standing against the wall was a large DVD storage shelf. Scanning the shelf, our pastor's attention began to focus on the numerous horror movies lined up in rows. "We must be mindful to close any open doors to the enemy," he encouraged. "These movies are welcoming the presence of fear in your home." The family didn't realize they were inviting spiritual darkness into their home under the facade of entertainment. Where do we think the creators of these horror movies get their diabolical ideas? From God? No! 2 Timothy 1:7 (NKJV) says, "For God has not given us a spirit of fear, but of power and of love and of a sound mind." Since God is not the originator of fear, where does it come from? Ephesians 6:12 (NKJV) says, "For we do not wrestle against flesh and blood, but against principalities, against powers, against the rulers of the darkness of this age, against spiritual hosts of wickedness in the heavenly places." Genuinely, there is a spiritual world of evil and fear is the fuel that runs this kingdom.

John 14:27 (NKJV), says "Peace I leave with you, My peace I give to you; not as the world gives do I give to you. Let not your heart be troubled, neither let it be afraid." Jesus was commanding us to not allow our hearts to fear. It is a choice to let fear enter our hearts. We must be very watchful to not promote opportunities that will spark fear in our children. As parents, we should be cautious to not associate fear with having fun. This is the reason Kevin and I had specific guidelines for Halloween. We did not prevent our children from dressing up in costumes, but they weren't allowed to wear scary or gruesome outfits. We would usually participate in our church's fall festival where they would play games and get plenty of candy. We shunned the fearful side of Halloween. It makes no sense to shield our children the best we can from scary things all year long, and yet on Halloween we pull out all the stops. Homes are decorated with tombstones, knives with fake blood, zombies, witches, Frankenstein, vampires, ghosts—the scarier the better, and we say, "Just for today, this is fun. Enjoy yourselves kids!"

Kevin and I were very diligent to guard our children from fear-provoking images and situations. We were even mindful about all of us watching murder case shows or unsolved mysteries about kids who were kidnapped. We closed any door we felt could feed fear in our children's hearts. Because of this, I don't ever remember any one of our children calling us to come to their room because they were afraid. Amazingly, they didn't have scary dreams because there wasn't a bunch of fear planted in their hearts and minds.

Irrational fears can unknowingly be instilled within children. I'm reminded of one of my daughter's friends who was a junior in high school at the time. She was an only child and her parents were quite protective of her. It was obvious that they were very consumed with their daughter and it seemed that the daughter was equally absorbed with her parents. After one of the events at school, I had an opportunity to speak with this girl's mother. I'm not sure how it came up, but she mentioned that her daughter had never been alone at home for any length of time. Although she was sixteen years old, her mother said she refused to be by herself. If the daughter was taking a nap and her mom said she was going to the grocery store for a few minutes, she would immediately pop up from a deep sleep and stumble out the door with her mom. Her mother said she wished she would have been more diligent during her daughter's middle-school years to give her opportunities to stay at home for small stints of time. Now that her daughter was older, she wasn't quite sure what to do. The mother had no clue that perhaps she and her husband had fostered an inordinate attachment with their daughter to the point where she could not function without them, and in fact, was fearful to not be with them. Of course, we know our children's limitations more than anyone else, but usually by the ages of twelve to thirteen our children should be able to stay at home by themselves for a few hours.

When I was a kid, my mom would never allow my sister or me to go in the front yard (EVER!), because she knew we would get kidnapped. We began to believe it, too! Some children are petrified to venture out because parents have made them afraid of everyone and everything. We have to be wise and not put our children in potentially dangerous situations, but we can do this without instilling fear in them. Romans 8:14 (NLV) says, "For all who are led by the Spirit of God are children of God." Our focus should be training our children to be led by the Spirit of God and His peace, not by fear. We must be cognizant of any type of fears—real or imagined—that may try to creep into our children's lives, and stop them in their tracks!

James 4:7 (NKJV) says, "Therefore submit to God. Resist the devil and he will flee from you." It's our job to resist the devil, which means we should be resisting the fear he brings our way. We can't ask our children to embrace or cuddle up to fear in one moment, and yet stand firm against it in another.

Fear is fear no matter how we look at it. Fear is not a friend but an enemy, and it must be treated as such. Fearful images can take root in a child's mind and in their subconscious, ever ready to be played out and bleed into their reality. It's important to ask ourselves, "Will this build my child's faith, or will it build fear in them?"

Our arrows will certainly lose equilibrium when fear infiltrates their lives. Starving fear from their hearts will allow them to be single-minded as they courageously move toward their target with unhindered purpose.

## Christmas Traditions

I love the peace found on Christmas day. It's the one day of the year where the hustle and bustle of life is allowed to temporarily halt, giving way to focus on faith, friends, and family. Grocery stores, which are usually open any other day of the year, are locked and silent. A few gas stations are open, but in general a holy hush falls upon our communities. The smell of nutmeg and cinnamon fills the air of our home in those early morning hours—it's my husband's famous French toast casserole loaded with enough butter, cream, and brown sugar to make even the most disciplined dieter drool! Our family gathers together and reads a treasured storybook called *The Christmas Lizard* that was purchased many years ago by my mother when Austin was first born. It is about an iguana who explores his way up through a Christmas tree while meeting many ornaments who think they know what the real meaning of Christmas is. He finally meets an angel at the top of the tree who shares the story of Jesus's birth with him. As the story comes to an end, we then clasp hands as a family and shift our attention to prayer and thanksgiving to Jesus Christ, Savior of the world. He is the greatest gift that was and ever will be given to us. We are quick to acknowledge that "every good and perfect gift comes from above, coming down from the Father of the heavenly lights, who does not change like shifting shadows" (James 1:17, NIV). We thank our Father for blessing us with the presents we are about to open and in a flash, we begin to methodically rip the beautifully wrapped paper off the gifts marked with our names. Welcome to our Schafer family Christmas morning tradition!

Traditions are important because they unveil what is important to us as a family, solidify our bond, and create memories that can span through the generations. Traditions don't have to be elaborate. In our case, a simple story, prayer, and breakfast on Christmas morning is extremely meaningful to us.

Kevin and I chose to focus on Christmas being Jesus's birthday. We told our children that because it was His birthday, we would celebrate by opening gifts. They were always happy to receive their presents and toys knowing that those things were a special blessing from God to them.

We know wonderful Christian families who have chosen to heavily incorporate Santa in their Christmas tradition, but we decided not to put the emphasis on him. Our pastor said that some things are neither right nor wrong, they are just different. I believe this is one of those traditions. Our kid's beliefs in Santa were ignited by their interactions with friends and by watching Christmas movies. We didn't squelch their belief, but we did not make a grand deal about Santa. Our main focus was on Jesus's birthday.

I have witnessed some parents "milking" Santa for all he's worth in order to manipulate their kids into being good during the Christmas season. It is unnerving to hear the broken record responses from parents in December: "You better be good because Santa is watching." "Do you want to get coal in your stocking?" "Do you want any presents from Santa? You'd better straighten up!" In all actuality, our children should behave whether Santa Claus comes to town or not. Honoring and respecting their parents and their Heavenly Father should be their main motivation, not a white bearded guy in a red suit checking his list for their name. Armed with that truth, our kids can miraculously behave all year long. Now that's a gift that keeps on giving!

Christmas traditions, as well as any family ritual throughout the year, will be a trusted constant for our children. These symbolic moments will bind our families together, bringing with them a stability our arrows need to course steadily through the tests of time.

## Respect and Honor

My southern roots go deep and most children in the South are raised to say "ma'am" and "sir," even to their parents! When I moved to Indiana at nine years old, I realized not every kid was taught to do so. I believe this type of behavior is about respect and not region. In a society where dishonor abounds, we must be diligently proactive in fostering honor whenever and wherever we can with our children.

Looking people in the eye when we are speaking or being spoken to is also an important form of respect. Guiding our children to look up from their phones and give someone their full attention shows they are listening, engaged, and value the conversation. Making a point to be assertively friendly and inquiring about another's life and wellbeing is very respectful and are great lessons to teach our children. These interactions would also include wait staff at restaurants or cashiers at retail outlets. Remember they are people, too, whom Jesus bled and died for! Standing up in the room to greet an elder or someone in leadership is another way to give honor. This may seem overthe-top, but I think about John 13:1-7 where Jesus washed his disciple's feet. Jesus should have been the one having his feet washed, but He chose to serve and honor extravagantly. As Christians, we don't just have a choice to honor and respect others, but we have a responsibility to do so.

Authentic respect and honor begins at home. Our children should never be allowed to boss us around by saying, "Get me this!" or "I need that!" "Would you please bring me ___?" or "May I have ___?" are much better phrases. "Please" and "thank you," preferring others, not insisting on our own way, letting others take the lead, and allowing kindness to be our guide go very far, not just at home but in life. I think we can all vouch that being nice and sweet rather than rude and demanding to people usually paves the way for more successful encounters. Children can at a very young age, with consistent direction and correction, begin to grasp the importance of being kind and respectful.

If we breed a culture of honor and respect, it will become a natural inclination within our children. Every one of our kids have the capacity to become world-changing leaders. It won't be a title or position that catapults them to great heights but the attitude of their hearts and how they honor and respect others.

Romans 13:7 (TLB) says, " . . . give honor and respect to all those to whom it is due." Respect and honor contain strategic counterbalancing measures to overcome the relentless temptation to mock, ridicule, and demean others. Seizing opportunities to bless and esteem someone, will pull our arrows back into alignment to successfully complete their mission.

CHAPTER THREE

# ARROWS MUST BE SHARP

An arrow without an arrowhead is only a stick. The arrowhead is the crowning jewel, and without it the arrow would never fulfill its purpose in reaching and piercing a target. When the bow is drawn back and the arrow shaft is released, the momentum and full force of that power is focused into the tiny point of the arrowhead. The depth of penetration and the amount of damage inflicted depends largely on the sharpness of that arrowhead. An arrow shaft can be constructed from the fi nest wood or carbon with a phenomenal balancing system, but none of this matters if the arrowhead is dull.

Maintaining a razor edge in their spirits and in everyday life, will allow our children to smoothly cut through obstacles that would normally seem impenetrable. Our child's sensitivity can easily be dulled, but there are things we can do as parents to protect their sharpness and ability to perform at maximum capacity.

**Love Your Spouse**

"Daddy, will you please come home with us?" my little sister and I pleaded. We had been tasked by our mother with a very important family mission—*Operation Bring Dad Home*. Packing a small bag of clothes and toiletries, Dad would frequently move out of the house to stay at his family-run insurance office after fiery arguments with mom. Hearing the familiar slam of the front door closing I held my breath wondering, "Is it the end this time?" On high alert, I was ready when called upon by Mom to put on my best smile and give my tightest hug to hopefully coax my dad to come to his senses and return to his family. Fortunately, Dad never hesitated to say "yes." On cue, my sister and I would erupt with exuberant cheers while Mom and Dad inched forward to seal the moment with a kiss. We had succeeded once again! Living with the constant threat of divorce, the emotional roller coaster I was riding was neither amusing nor entertaining. When my parents finally did end their marriage, although sad, I was surprisingly relieved.

The honeymoon season was short-lived after my mom married my stepfather. Extreme financial pressure took its toll on their marriage and heated battles began to rage again within our home. In a flash, I returned to my reserved seat on the roller coaster from hell with all its unexpected dips, turns, and plummeting dives!

My parent's constant turmoil and opposition pushed them closer and closer to the edge of divorce. Although dissolving a marriage may be common in this day age, with around fifty percent of married couples impacted, it is not God's best. Because we are imperfect people with the ability to make choices according to our free wills, God does make allowances for divorce. However, it should be a last resort and not a knee-jerk reaction when going through marital challenges. In Amy Desai, J.D.'s article "Who Gets Divorced?" she says, "Research shows the majority of marriages ending in divorce have average levels of happiness and conflict. In other words, these are not deeply troubled, physically or emotionally abusive relationships, although even those are not always irreversibly broken. In short, most of the marriages that end in divorce are just plain average, or "good enough." Instead of throwing in the towel, these average marriages could be improved over time—if the spouses stayed together."

Insanity is doing the same thing over and over again and expecting different results. Sometimes we just need a fresh perspective and game plan to get our marriages back on track. God specializes in the reconstruction business. He can take our messes and make something magnificent! Faith-based counselors are an excellent resource to help us sort through the rubble and find what's valuable again. Multitudes of books, seminars, classes, podcasts, and videos exist to equip us with tools for steadily growing as husband and wife. Disagreements about money are one of the main causes of divorce. Dave Ramsey's *Financial Peace University* is a great resource for practical ways of taking control of our finances, paying off debt, and saving money. Linking together with a mature believer or spiritual leader for accountability is a sure way to enhance the quality of our marriages. Our relationship is worth the investment! Answers are available and if we are willing to put in the work, most of our marriages can be saved. Laid at the Heavenly Father's feet, He can repair and restore even the direst of situations. We have the ability through Christ to push through and show our children how to build love that lasts.

After twenty-nine years of marriage, my husband and I have put some guidelines into place to not only protect our relationship but also to build family security in our children. We make a point to outwardly display our devotion and love for each other in front of our children. We hug. We kiss. (We don't go totally crazy, now—we keep it classy!) We hold hands and we laugh together. We show our kids that not only do we love each other, but we LIKE each other, too! Do we have disagreements at times? Of course! Who doesn't? When those times come, if at all possible, work things out in private away from earshot of the kids. If things get a little heated in front of our children, it's important to apologize. "Would you please forgive us for the way we were speaking to each other?" or "We didn't honor each other by acting that way, and we are sorry you had to see that" will help diffuse any potential break-up fears seeking to take root in their hearts.

Ephesians 4:26-27 (NIV) says, "In your anger do not sin": Do not let the sun go down while you are still angry and do not give the devil a foothold." Not speaking to one another for days at a time is dangerous territory, and it opens the door to the enemy for all kinds of trouble. Therefore, it is very destructive on our relationships if we go to bed angry with each other. In all honesty, neither of us sleep soundly when we're angry, so we may as well get up and talk things through. Kevin and I have developed a very effective strategy we call the *toe* ministry. We may be the only ones this has happened to (Ha!), but if we find ourselves in bed and in disagreement, we may be tempted to move to the side of our mattress and teeter on the edge where we almost roll off. In order for our mate to realize how upset we are, we have to prevent touching them or even feeling the heat of their body, and by all means, NO SPEAKING! It is at this point that one of us will muster up enough courage to swing out our foot and lightly touch the other person's leg with our toe. It is like the proverbial olive branch of peace. It's a powerful icebreaker and before long we are in each other's arms working through the disagreement in unity. Go ahead and try it. The toe ministry works!

Repetitive cycles of arguing, bitterness, humiliation, and anger between parents, take their toll upon the hearts of children.

Their tender spirits can easily be dulled by the constant pain of seeing their parents at odds. One of the most powerful things we can do for our children is to love our spouse. A stable and nurturing relationship between a husband and wife gives our arrows the cutting edge to penetrate their destinies with confident assurance.

## Four Ways of Dealing with Divorce

With a smirk on his face, Dad handed my sister and me each a container that looked like a soup can. We were in the midst of opening presents for Christmas, so this took us a little off guard. "There's a surprise in it, but you have to open it with a can opener." It was just like Dad to do something creative and fun and we were thoroughly enjoying our visit with him over the holiday break. With great anticipation we watched the can opener round the lid, and with every spin of the handle we grew closer and closer to seeing the secret prize inside. As the tops came off, my sister and I reached inside our "canned gifts" and pulled out a crisp one hundred dollar bill. In the early 1980s one hundred dollars was a lot of money, especially for two little girls. Dad said we could put our money in a savings account, or go to the mall and buy whatever we wanted. It was a no-brainer for us. We could not wait to burn through our money and shop 'til we dropped! The evening after our "haul," my sister and I excitedly called our mother to share the treasures we had purchased. Our exuberance was soon dashed as Mom began to express her opposition to the two pairs of expensive tennis shoes my little sister bought. She questioned their practicality and was not happy that our father did not intervene with proper guidance for a first-grader. Dad rushed to the phone and within minutes an ugly argument ensued. When Dad hung up the phone, the flood gates of animosity opened up and he and my stepmother began a lengthy tirade of negativity about my mother. Hurtful details about her and my parent's previous relationship were painstakingly unveiled. I sat there trapped, unable to dodge the relentless barrage of hostility. Every hateful blow was targeted to push me into my father's corner, but I stood my ground. In the angry, charged atmosphere I was smart enough not to speak, but my heart was determined to never betray my mother. Knowing she had no voice to defend herself, my love became her invisible shield of protection. What was meant to repel me from my mom thrust me closer than I had ever been. The next day my sister and I boarded the airplane to go back home. I clearly remember dryly hugging my father as we said our goodbyes, and making a solemn pledge to never speak to him again. I made good on that promise for the next seven years.

When divorce happens it is painful for everyone involved, especially children. If we're not careful, they can become innocent casualties caught in the crossfire of relationship battles. My father's and my relationship suffered extreme damage. Thankfully, God was able to bridge our hearts together again, but a lot of precious years were wasted. It is possible to protect children from needless harm in the tumultuous times of divorce. Following are four ways to create safe boundaries for them:

### 1.  Honor An Ex-Spouse

Ephesians 6:2-3 (KJV) says, "Honor your father and mother," which is the first commandment with promise: "that it may be well with you and you may live long on the earth." This verse is not a suggestion to honor our parents—it is a commandment. Honoring them is not contingent on whether we feel they are deserving of it. If divorce has taken place, how do we help our children honor an ex-spouse, so they may receive the promise of long life and things going well with them? A primary way to do that is very simple. Don't speak ill of an ex-spouse in front of your children and don't allow your children to say anything bad about them, even if your ex-spouse has passed away.

In Genesis 9:18-23, we read that Noah got drunk and passed out naked in his tent. Ham, Noah's youngest son, peeked into the tent and saw his father in this precarious position. He immediately went to tell his older brothers, Shem and Japheth. The scripture doesn't say what Ham told them, but one could imagine it went something like "Hey guys, you ought to see Dad right now. He got so soused that he fell out in the tent and he doesn't have a stitch of clothes on! He looks absolutely ridiculous!" Instead of Shem and Japheth chiming in with their brother to mock their father, they held a cloak between them and walked backwards to cover their father's nakedness. They even kept their faces turned away, so they did not see his nude body!

When Noah awoke and realized that Ham had disgraced and dishonored him, he was furious. He immediately pronounced blessings upon Shem and Japheth, and a curse upon Ham. Ham missed out on God's blessing because he chose to expose his father in a weakened state. Honoring our parents is serious business with God! Proverbs 20:20 (TPT) says, "If you despise your father or mother, your life will flicker out like a lamp, extinguished into the deepest darkness."

Steering our personal and our children's conversations to speak well of an ex-spouse may be challenging, but it will bring great reward. Painful interactions with an exspouse can close the mind so that it focuses only on the negative aspects of their character. We must remember that in spite of any shortcomings, everyone has redeeming and positive qualities. Most of us were drawn to something good in our mates or ex-spouses, or we would not have married them. If not cautious, divorcees can begin to perceive the ex-spouse as the enemy and adopt an "us against them" mentality. This mindset bleeds into and violates the parent-child relationship.

Dishonoring an ex-spouse will only tear down, destroy, and hinder the entire family from going forward. Showing our children how to honor both parents, whether deserved or undeserved, will open up untold avenues of God's blessing.

## 2.  Have Private Conversations with An Ex-Spouse

Guarding children from difficult conversations with or about an ex-spouse will protect them from having to filter nonessential, potentially upsetting information. When children hear problems concerning them or their parents' relationship, they start making judgment calls internally on who's right or wrong. A child's point of view can be skewed and they normally magnify the negativity of the situation. To protect children from any possible mental distress, tough discussions should be handled privately, away from their ears. The conversation should end immediately with a promise to connect later, if privacy is not an option.

## 3.  Pray for An Ex-Spouse

Seize opportunities to pray with your children about your ex-spouse, asking God to bring about His love and light into their lives. Children should sense a genuineness that the welfare and spiritual progress of an ex-spouse is important, though they may have caused the family great pain. We can demonstrate how to love someone who may seem unlovable at the moment.

We should not portray to our children that we are the "better" parent in any situation. This is equally true of non

Christian ex-spouses. Without the amazing love of Jesus, we would all be destined for hell. We should never want that for anyone, especially for the parent of our children.

Closing children off from an ex-spouse because they are not a believer won't draw them any closer to God. It will most likely push them further away from Him. Though it may seem easier to let the relationship slide, do your best to foster meaningful interactions between your children and ex-spouse. As your children grow older, they will be very appreciative of any efforts to help them maintain and value strong ties with their parent.

If it is unsafe for children to be around an ex-spouse, details about their indiscretions need not be told. Communicate information that is necessary and beneficial for children. When they are young, very little information needs to be shared at all. Some secrets about ex-spouses need to be taken to the grave. Disclosing intimate details of their dirty laundry to children, even as adults, is shameful and needless.

James 5:16 (TPT) says, "Confess and acknowledge how you have offended one another [ and then pray for one another to be instantly healed, for tremendous power is released through the passionate, heartfelt prayer of a godly believer!"

Prayer softens our hearts and paves the way for restoration. When we allow God to intervene on our behalf, He is able to bring healing to the deepest and darkest areas of our lives. Including our children on this prayer journey will ignite hope in their hearts and bring comfort to any loss they may be experiencing.

## 4.  Walk in Forgiveness with An Ex-Spouse

For seven long years I fed the flame of unforgiveness against my dad. I clung to the bitterness by rehearsing the story again and again of why I deserved to feel the way I did. It was my senior year of high school and I couldn't believe Dad had never reached out to me once since our Christmas feud in 1980. I was his child, for Heaven's sake, and he obviously could care less about me. I had become accustomed to hating my father for the way he spoke about my mother, and the anger was eating me up on the inside. I had rededicated my life to Christ over the past year and the Holy Spirit began to deal with me to make things right with Dad. God opened my eyes to His love for my father, and showed me that my lack of forgiveness was hindering Dad from receiving that love. Suddenly it wasn't just about me anymore and the pain I had experienced. Now it was about a living, breathing soul who needed the touch from a compassionate savior. I'll never forget the day I picked up the phone to call my dad. It felt like a hundred-pound brick, but I made myself dial his number. When I heard Dad's voice, all I could say was "Dad, I'm sorry" and uncontrollable tears began to fall. Those three simple words instantly crumbled the offense and pain I had held on to for so long. Forgiveness was the key that unlocked my self-inflicted chains. Hearing my dad's sobs on the other end of the phone, I knew that he was free, too.

Maybe our wounds and our bitterness seem justified by the actions of an ex-spouse. Perhaps they inflicted the most intense pain ever experienced. In the end, we are the ones imprisoned by our own unyielding hatred. I have heard the phrase that unforgiveness is like drinking poison yourself and waiting for the other person to die. It's a slow death that erodes our purpose, our passion, and our pursuit of all God has for us. For every toxic sip of offense, forgiveness is the antidote.

> *Lay aside bitter words, temper tantrums, revenge, profanity, and insults. But instead be kind and affectionate toward one another. Has God graciously forgiven you? Then graciously forgive one another in the depths of Christ's love.*
>
> —Ephesians 4:31-32 (TPT)

> *And whenever you stand praying, if you find that you carry something in your heart against another person, release him and forgive him, so that your Father in heaven will also release you and forgive you of your faults.*
>
> —Mark 11:25 (TPT)

When we hold unforgiveness in our heart, it can hinder our prayers.

God showed me the exact steps to take in order to make amends with my dad. He may lead us to call an ex-spouse and ask for forgiveness. He may direct us to release the anger and begin praying for the ex-spouse as a brother or sister in Christ. When we've obliterated the walls of our lack of forgiveness, we give God permission to turn our greatest losses into miraculous triumphs. Making a commitment to forgive an ex-spouse sets the atmosphere for children to confidently thrive.

The end of a marriage doesn't have to be the beginning of a child's downfall. Commitment as husband and wife may be over, but responsibility as parents remains intact. Children can still maintain a sense of stability by seeing unified parents who resist the temptation to disrespect one another. The choice to get along and sincerely care about the other's well-being sharpens and refines our arrows to smoothly punch through any target ahead.

## You Can't Put a Price Tag on Peace

Coming off the school bus, I listened to the crunch of the gravel under my feet as I walked the long driveway to my house. I scanned the yard and took in all of the activity taking place on our property. As usual, the farm was buzzing with pickup trucks, tractors, trailers, skid loaders, men with work gloves, and cats galore. The smell of hay mixed with the pungent odor of cow manure was hovering in the air. At the time, my stepfather owned one of the largest and most prestigious dairy farms in the world. Taking the few stairs up the stoned porch, I opened the beautiful golden brown oak door with its familiar creak. I inched cautiously through the entry hall and listened intently. My stepfather's home office was directly to my right. Was it too silent? Did I hear laughter? Did I hear yelling or soft intense whispers? I knew right away if my parents were having a good day or a bad one. Unfortunately, most days were the bad ones. My best line of defense was to stay "invisible" and not make any waves. If I needed to ask them a question, I would first evaluate it to make sure it was absolutely important enough to bring up. I had learned to be very choosy in asking for anything because their stress level was so high, even the smallest of things could become the tipping point for a major blow up. It seemed as if it were burdensome for me to ask them to stay at a friend's house or drive me anywhere, that I began feeling guilty for even asking. They had so many things on their plate that I did not want to add to their stress level.

As the eldest of five children (one sister from my mom's first marriage and three siblings from my mother's second marriage), my parents consistently confided in me about their financial, marital, and legal challenges. I wanted to be a good daughter, so I offered a listening ear and stepped in to be a sounding board. In some ways I felt important that they would tell me their behind-the-scenes business, but knowing so much weighed heavy on my heart. After I moved out of the house and got married, the drama continued and so did my coveted position of family confidante. I would get so stressed-out hearing the pain in my mother's voice and seeing my stepfather wearily juggling a failing business. I would pray, but I had this overwhelming sense of responsibility that somehow I needed to come up with a solution to their problems.

When my husband and I had been married about ten years, the arguing and turmoil between my parents reached a new high. We suddenly had a eureka moment. As bad as we hated being involved with all of the family chaos, we had been willing participants. I will never forget a heart-to-heart conversation with my parents where I told them I no longer wanted to hear their business, marriage, or financial woes again. I was kind but explained that even though I was an adult now, I was still their child and there were just some things that shouldn't be shared with me. I expressed how much I loved them, but Kevin and I were drawing a boundary from that day forward of how we would be interacting with them. It was a wake-up call to them and things did get better. Once we removed ourselves from all the negative and chaotic talk, sadly we didn't have much to talk about during that season of life.

Not long afterwards, Kevin and I had an opportunity to move to Pittsburgh, Pennsylvania to help my husband's brother and wife pioneer a church. Austin was three years old and our first daughter, Kamryn, was about six months old. We felt the leading of the Lord to go. It was a long way from Oklahoma where we had been living with my family.

The move to Pittsburgh was one of the best decisions we have ever made. It allowed our children to grow up in an environment where they didn't have to regularly encounter chaos, pressure, and strife. They have never had to deal with a constant sickness in their stomach or feeling on edge as they try to tune out the shouts of those they love. Instead, they were able to focus on the things that really matter most like their relationship with the Lord, their relationships with each other, and their studies. They were able to focus on their dreams and hopes and not stresses of constant disagreements and negativity. The move also allowed my husband and me to focus on parenting our children, and the things God was calling us to do. We were no longer being swept away by impromptu family drama that was virtually sucking the life out of us.

I made a promise to myself that whenever I was married and had children, our home would be a home filled with peace. Our home is a no-drama zone. We don't let the sun go down on our wrath (Ephesians 4:26). We work things out respectfully and kindly. We pursue peace. We don't just hope peace comes to our home. We run after it.

Romans 14:19 says, "Let us therefore make every effort to do what leads to peace and to mutual edification." This passage says to make EVERY effort to do what leads to peace and boy, does it ever take effort! If one way doesn't work, try another way, and then another. We should do whatever we can to have peace. Now, some may say that peace is agreement. This passage doesn't say that. It says make every effort to do what leads to peace, not agreement.

We will have many opportunities to agree to disagree, but we can still have peace if we make it a priority!

Unfortunately, friction can occur between our parents and their ideas of how we should raise our children. If not dealt with quickly and correctly, these issues can cause marital problems between us and our spouse. We must realize that when it comes to parenting, some things aren't wrong but only a preference. If we are raising our children in the admonition of the Lord, we don't have to feel guilty by taking the lead as a parent. We can lovingly thank our parents for their input, but explain that we are going to do things a little differently. Hopefully, they are willing to respect our wishes and boundaries. Nevertheless, we should be encouraged that we pursued peace and resolution in the moment.

Peace doesn't necessarily mean a still, quiet environment. Life can be clipping along at a steady pace, but we don't have to be awkwardly walking on pins and needles with each other, speaking sharply to one another, being in constant disagreement with each other, or participating in habitual negativity. God's peace is like a cocoon of rest. No matter what is going on, we can always have a sense of inner peace and well-being.

Setting a peaceful atmosphere in our home is one of the most important decisions we can make. Kevin and I play Christian music in our home all day long, even when we are not home. When we go on vacation, we keep the Christian radio on. Why do we do that? We are intentionally setting the environment for God's peace and presence to abide in our home.

Colossians 3:15 (NIV) says, "Let the peace of Christ rule in your hearts, since as members of one body you were called to peace." God has called us to peace. He is saying, "Hey come over here! Come over to peace! This is where I want you to be!" We should not purposefully put ourselves in situations that steal our peace. Let's avoid drama like the plague!

We are the captain of our own ship. We really can pick and choose what we want to do and whom we are going to do it with. Don't drop the anchor at drama's dock. Set our course for peace!

We can't put a price tag on peace. We can give our kids all kinds of things, but the greatest gift we can give them is the ability to experience God's peace in their everyday lives. That peace brings a clarity to hear the Lord's voice and knock off any rough edges meant to slow down the progress of our arrows.

## Never Let Your Children Leave Home Angry

It happens. Our children are just about to walk out the door and World War III breaks loose. Maybe our daughters are fighting over who gets to wear the black pair of flats, or our son can't find his favorite jacket. Perhaps we've just said no to an impromptu sleepover, and our child's life is now ruined.

When our children are upset and worked up into a frenzy, that is not the time to let them head out of the house to go to school or to any event. James 3:16 (KJV) says, "For where envying and strife is, there is confusion and every evil work."

Chaos, dissension, and confusion are open doors to the devil. He thrives in these types of arenas. Several times I kept one or all of my children home from a class period, or two, of school until they cooled down. If we said words that weren't right to each other, we would make amends and apologize. We'd pray together, ask God's forgiveness, and make sure all was well between us. It is of the utmost importance to send our children out with peace in their hearts. It's also amazing—once they realize we will make good on our promise to keep them home— how quickly they can dial back their attitudes!

I have the privilege to serve on staff at our church in the Member Care department. Many of the calls we receive are from people in crisis who need prayer support. I will never forget a call from a grieving mother whose teenage son died in a tragic car accident. She and her son had gotten into an argument at home and she yelled for him to "just get out of here." He tore out of the driveway in a fit of rage, and in that chaotic mindset ended up wrecking his car and losing his life. This mother not only had to cope with the death of her son, but also knew that her thoughtless angered words were a catalyst in the outcome.

John 10:10 (NKJV) says, "The thief does not come except to steal, and to kill, and to destroy." The devil is looking for any opportunity to bring destruction to our families. We should not give him any ammunition to use. It may be inconvenient, but giving our children time to get into a peaceful state of mind could literally save their lives.

I have found several practical things that have helped my children get out the door with ease:

### 1.  Make Enough Time to Get Ready

Quite possibly the number one reason for a chaotic morning is not allowing ourselves and our family enough time to get ready. Hitting the snooze over and over again is not the recipe for a successful day. We are just asking for chaos.

Some children need more time to wake up. We know our children and what is best for them. Give them ample time to wake up, have some breakfast, and have a simple prayer time with us or by themselves as they get older. Also, we may need to go to bed earlier in order to wake up earlier. We should get in the habit of having a regular bedtime for our children. It can be rough, but the payoff is great.

## 2.  Choose Clothes the Night Before

Choosing our children's clothes the night before helps offset a lot of stress. I have seen parents who pick out their children's clothes for the week. I never did that, but it's a fabulous idea. Picking out their church clothes the night before service will also add some peace of mind to those hectic Sunday mornings. On a side note, once children are in elementary school, they should be able to choose their own clothes. With a little guidance, they will do well with this responsibility.

## 3.  Have a Home for the Backpacks

Lots of time can be wasted running around looking for backpacks, homework, signed papers for the teachers, and pencils. We need to get those backpacks together with all their school items the night before. We should set them in the same area so they're ready to go.

## 4.  Let Your Kids Make Their Lunches

From an early age, my children made their own lunches before school or the night before. I purchased the sandwich items, fruit, yogurts, chips, etc. and they were responsible for putting it all together in their lunch boxes. The burden wasn't on me to make their lunches and they did a great job with their daily duty. Remember we are raising our children to be functioning, responsible adults. We won't always be around to make their lunches!

## 5.  Know When Those Projects Are Due

How about those last-minute school projects? Keeping abreast of our children's homework will help some of those ball drops. The more children we have, the more difficult this is. I wasn't perfect at it, but I tried.

We must do our best to not allow our children to procrastinate until the day before projects are due. We are just asking for drama. There is nothing more frustrating than making a trip to Wal-Mart in the middle of the night for pipe cleaners or a presentation folder. We should show our children how beneficial wise planning can be when it comes to their schoolwork.

## 6.  Have Timely Conversations

Here's a great tip! We should not bring things up that we know may upset them right before our child walks out the door. No one is more aware of our children's hot topics than us. We should plan for serious discussions when their minds are fresh and we have time to do the topic justice. We shouldn't try and cram a thirty-minute exchange into a ten-minute drive to school, or rush to talk about a bad grade two minutes before our teenager is leaving to attend their school choir practice. This inevitably brings frustration to us and our kids. By all means, we should not have difficult conversations with our children via text message. Face-to-face is always best, so nothing can be miscommunicated by not being able to see each other's body language or hear the inflections in each other's voices. When there is a serious conversation, be deliberate. We shouldn't just come out of the gate without any direction. We should plan ahead what we would like to address and what the goal of the conversation will be. When we do talk, we should remain calm and stay on track with the purpose of the conversation. Proverbs 12:18 (AMPC) says, "There are those who speak rashly, like the piercing of a sword, but the tongue of the wise brings healing." We should resist the knee-jerk reaction to deal with a situation in the wrong moment. It can usually wait!

## 7. Keep Your Cool

We must recognize when a situation is starting to get out of hand. Raising our voice only elevates things and doesn't bring us any closer to a solution. We have the ability to bring a calm and peace into a situation before it spins out of control. Proverbs 26:20 (CEV) says, "Where there is no fuel a fire goes out." A simple "Hey, it's going to be okay" or "I love you, son. I am for you more than anyone else in this world" can help extinguish the sparks of a potential inferno.

## 8. Listen to Your Children

When we listen to our children and not cut them off right away, it paves the way for peace. Sometimes we exasperate our kids by not hearing their full perspective. Proverbs 18:13 (NLT) says, "Spouting off before listening to the facts is both shameful and foolish." Even if we don't agree with their train of thought, hearing them out can help them feel respected and validated.

If we don't have the time to properly discuss a matter before our child leaves, look them in the eye and say, "What you have to say is really important to me. I don't want to rush talking about this because we are on a tight schedule. Let's talk about this tonight, okay?" Be sure and talk about it that night or whatever time you agreed upon. Handling things this way is a win/win situation. Our children can be assured we are listening, and we will be able to give them our full attention at a later time.

## 9. Loosen Up

Everything doesn't have to be so serious. In the heat of a moment, I've been known to pause and just start dancing in front of my kids. It injected a little bit of humor into the situation and before we knew it, we were all laughing and forgot what we were arguing about. We usually end in hugs, realizing the mild rift wasn't worth the effort any more.

Anger flare-ups can easily be prevented if we heed the warning signs. When heated moments begin to roll in, God's love in us can dissipate the fiercest of clouds before a storm breaks loose. Avoiding strife in our homes will defend our arrows from enemy attacks sent to wreak havoc on their emotions and dull their performance spiritually, mentally, and physically.

## Guard Your Heart

"Hey Mom, what's for lunch? I'm hungry!" I exclaimed. In eager anticipation I watched Mom grab the soft white Wonder Bread out of the blue, red, and yellow dotted white plastic bag. The butter knife clinked in the glass Miracle Whip jar as she generously doused two slices of bread with the delicious goodness. Carefully, she removed the thin plastic red strip casing around the generous cut of bologna and placed it on the bread. Finally, she took off the clear cellophane from the American cheese and sat it on top of the sandwich as the crowning jewel. And voila, there was my lunch! If I was lucky, I would get a Hostess Ding Dong or Twinkie for dessert. In this day and age many parents would cringe at the thought of giving their child a meal like this. We are armed with much better nutritional information and are more mindful as to what is going into our bodies. Some parents are extremely watchful to the point of restricting their children from dyes, artificial flavorings, and going gluten-free, dairy-free, and nut-free. Why would we go to such lengths? The bottom line is we want our children to be as healthy as possible.

It's great parenting to ensure our kids aren't eating a bunch of junk, but there is one thing that deserves the most care of all, and that is their hearts. Proverbs 4:23 (CSB) says, "Guard your heart above all else, for it is the source of life." The Passion Translation says, "… Pay attention to the welfare of your innermost being, for from there flows the wellspring of life." Although we want our children's bodies healthy, our greatest focus should be the well-being, safety, and protection of their spirit man. Everything they will ever become and any impact they will ever have in this world stems from what is or isn't allowed into their hearts. A child's heart is extremely valuable, and guarding it takes careful and persistent work and effort.

The entry points into a child's heart are their ear-gates and eye-gates. Whatever they see and whatever they hear will greatly affect the course and direction of their lives. Music, movies, video games, television shows, and social media can be tremendous influencers. With all of the music and media options, it may seem overwhelming to have to screen through all of this material. In my opinion, it is one of the most challenging aspects of parenting. We are usually swimming upstream from society and unfortunately, many families—including fellow Christians—that we encounter will not be as vigilant about protecting their children from harmful heart-altering junk.

I was in fourth grade and disco fever was in the air. Donna Summer, The Bee Gees, and Sister Sledge were the hot artists of the day, and John Travolta's Saturday Night Fever was a box office hit. One of my friends from school asked if I would like to go see the movie with her and her mom. Since it was such a popular dance movie, my mom said it would be fine to go. I fully expected the movie to be an hour and a half of watching cool dance moves and having fun, but that wasn't exactly what I saw. I witnessed and heard the moans and groans of a couple having sex in the back of a moving car, another scene of a woman getting raped, and several nude images. I felt dirty and violated, like I had seen something I could never unsee again. I was also fire-hosed by a barrage of foul language. I recently looked up the movie on an onsite parental guide and this is what I heard that night: Around 80 uses of the f-word, 35 uses of "s—t"", 4 uses of "c—k", 3 uses of "ba—rd", 5 uses of "b—ch", 9 uses of "h—", 4 uses of "d—n", 14 uses of "a—", 4 uses of God's name paired with "d—n", multiple uses of "pu—y", and 14 uses of racist slang.

I apologize if that was hard to read but it's reality. These are the kinds of things our kids can be subjected to under the guise of a fun and hip movie. Unfortunately, our society can get so wrapped up in the coolest movie to hit the scene, that we open our mouths like helpless baby birds and take the worm. We willingly pay money for these "entertaining" experiences, not realizing our hearts are taking the blows of every image and sting of profanity. And, many families are watching these types of movies together at home or on a family outing!

As parents we may think, "Our kids can handle it. This won't impact them. This doesn't ultimately contribute to who they are as a person. Everyone is seeing this. It's no big deal. It's popular. It's a classic." Our children may know their moral boundaries, but for the sake of entertainment, why would we willingly allow them to watch people who are morally out of control? When we allow our children to be exposed to certain images of fear, violence, death, sexual situations, etc., what we are doing is allowing them to store up camera rolls in their mind, so to speak, that can be played out at any given time.

Galatians 6:7-8 (NASB) says, "Do not be deceived, God is not mocked; for whatever a man sows, this he will also reap. For the one who sows to his own flesh will from the flesh reap corruption, but the one who sows to the Spirit will from the Spirit reap eternal life." Everything allowed entry into our children's hearts are seeds being sown. My pastor, Scott Jones, says, "You will always harvest what you plant." If children view this type of material, it doesn't mean they won't go to Heaven, but there will be some type of repercussion for it being sown into their hearts. Because my parents were not diligent in helping me make the right viewing and listening choices, I had explicit images in my mind that fed into actions I reaped in high school and beyond. Many movies and music painted a deceptive picture of how I should be treated as a young lady, and what "loving" relationships looked like. I opened myself up to needless pain and drama because of the false images rooted in my heart.

Guarding our children's hearts from sexual images and foul language is important, but there are also other ways media can creep in to portray unhealthy scenarios.

## 1. Depictions of Young Love

If the channel kids are watching is geared toward preteens, it is highly likely many of the sitcom story lines focus on the guy winning a girl or vice versa. The young couple may end up in a loving embrace and kiss. These boys and girls are normally anywhere from ten to twelve years old. Images like these can foster a longing in our children to pursue relationships like this at an early age. They may sense that in order to be cool or feel special, it is necessary for them to have a boyfriend or girlfriend. Children are very impressionable, and they can grasp on to ideas quickly about how their world should operate. We decided it was best to have our children watch something else, even if it was a popular show.

After flipping through the first teen magazine we bought our girls, we soon realized many of the stories and advertisements were focused on "hot guys" and how to catch a boyfriend. We didn't want them meditating on these ideas, so we committed to no longer buying this material.

## 2. Disrespect—Comedic Use or Serious

Our children can pick up disrespectful behaviors by mimicking shows they are watching. Children dishonoring their parents for comedic emphasis is very popular on many programs. Usually, the parents stand in shock and say nothing as a dramatic pause is inserted for laughter from the audience. Siblings rudely reacting to each other is commonplace. Bickering between husbands and wives while putting each other down is also typical behavior. Cartoons are not exempt!

When children are continuously exposed to these types of actions, it may feed into a false belief of how a modern family should interact with one another.

## 3. Violence

Opening a child's heart to violent images, especially in video games is not wise. Technology has improved to the point where the video games are life-like, it is almost like players are characters on the screen. I personally feel that killing another human being is something that should be taken seriously and not portrayed in a game. War-time scenarios are the only thing that require such actions. Soldiers have undergone extensive training to be deemed the right to carry out those acts for the sake of our country. Arm-chair soldiers trivially portraying combat with their joysticks in the safety of their living rooms dishonor real soldiers who give their lives sacrificially each and every day to protect our country. Additionally, if a child is predisposed to aggression, violent movies and video games may feed into them crossing acceptable behavior boundary lines.

Depositing images of blood, gore, guts, and death into our children's heart accounts isn't going to be profitable for them in the long run. With a multitude of viewing options and video game choices, why not steer our children towards non-violent resources for their entertainment?

## 4. Female Dominance

It is my desire that my daughters sense a confidence and a boldness to achieve every dream God has placed in their hearts. However, there seems to be an all-out media siege against males in general. Television shows and movies promoting "girl power" are very popular. I am all for girl power, but I'm also for "boy power" for my son. The trend in today's media is to emasculate men, portraying them as bumbling idiots who can't do anything without a woman's direction. Usually, the wife is in control and dominates her husband. Female characters boss their foolish male friends around.

God has made males and females with different strengths and abilities. It's okay for boys to be confident, well-versed, and goal-oriented. It would be wonderful to see more big-screen, animated movies depicting strong, smart, purpose-filled boys and men. Girls are winning by a landslide in these films.

As parents, we should protect our boys from the idea that girls are superior to them. They do not need to apologize to anyone for being a man. Our girls should be taught it is not necessary to demean a man to get what they desire in life. Girls are not better than boys, and boys are definitely not better than girls. God treasures them both and His power in them is able to accomplish more than they could ever hope or dream.

## 5. Premature Death

Tearjerker movies and television shows are plentiful. We may have heard them classified as "chick flicks" or shows to watch when we want a good cry. The sadness behind them usually involves a main character dying prematurely or tragically. Perhaps the person is a child, a spouse, a good friend, or a girlfriend or boyfriend. The draw of movies is "going there" in our minds as we allow ourselves to identify with the characters being played. Although premature death may happen in this world, it's not God's best. I have spoken in detail about this in the chapters "Healer in the House" and "Sensitivity to the Holy Spirit."

Let's say we have allowed our children to feed on movies that romanticize young death. This can promote fears of them dying young or someone close to them passing away prematurely. I personally believe shows like this open their hearts to a slow erosion in their faith regarding God's promise of long life (Psalm 91:16). On the rare occasion of them receiving a bad report from the doctor, the last thing they need are etched images of lost battles with sickness to play out over and over in their minds.

I've noticed that in many of the animated movies, one or both parents are tragically killed prematurely and some of the children are left in the hands of a wicked stepparent. My children watched several of these animated shows, but it is something to note. One of my sisters brought her young daughter to see a popular animated film about a young fish and the character's mother was violently eaten at the beginning of the film by another sea creature. Needless to say, her daughter was so upset that they had to leave the movie.

As parents, we need to be mindful of exposing our children to "entertainment" portraying premature death. Guarding their hearts in this area is well worth the effort.

## 6. Suicide

Teen and preteen suicides have been rising at an alarming rate. According to the U.S. Centers for Disease Control and Prevention the following is true of youth:

- Suicide is the second leading cause of death for college-age youth and ages twelve to eighteen (2016).

- More teenagers and young adults die from suicide than from cancer, heart disease, AIDS, birth defects, stroke, pneumonia, influenza, and chronic lung disease COMBINED.

With this epidemic of self-inflicted harm based on seemingly hopeless circumstances, we must be very vigilant about guarding our children from ideas promoting suicide.

Currently there is a very successful teen drama on a streaming network about a high school girl who has taken her life. Each episode depicts flash backs of hurtful situations and people who contributed to her choice to commit suicide. Although the intention of this series was to open people's eyes to the harmful effects of bullying, some teens used the show to justify the decision to end their lives. Many of the preteen and teen girls I've seen in the news who recently committed suicide, did it by hanging themselves. The character on this show took her life by the same means and the act was depicted very graphically. I don't think it's coincidental.

As parents, we should not give the enemy any foothold in our children's lives by allowing images of glamorized self-destruction to enter their hearts. We must be watchful and aware that shows like this exist.

## 7.  Horror Movies

Horror movies offer a certain thrill and adrenaline rush that some people find very entertaining. Watching a murderous maniac or an evil presence wreaking havoc on an innocent person, gives substance to bone-chilling fears never thought possible. Once moviegoers experience that fear, producers know they must push beyond the boundaries into uncharted realms in order to satiate the unquenchable appetite to see something different. Fear will take as much ground as we are willing to give it. I focus much more on this subject in the chapter "Don't Feed Fears."

Psalm 101:3 (KJV) says, "I will set no wicked thing before my eyes." We should be diligent in preventing our children from purposely setting wicked things before their eyes and "playing with fear." Unfortunately, fear doesn't play fair and its objective is to take a bite out of them.

## 8.  Car and Fashion Magazines

One Easter Kevin and I had the idea of putting a car magazine in Austin's basket along with all of his other goodies. He is an avid car enthusiast and we knew he would enjoy leafing through the pages of custom vehicles. Thankfully, we did our own sifting through the car magazines before we bought one. Sprinkled throughout several pages were women scantily clad in skimpy bikinis or bosom-revealing outfits. We looked through a few other magazines and found some that didn't have all of the extra eye candy.

Fashion magazines are a big pull for teen girls. Unfortunately, many of the images and poses are extremely sexualized and border on soft porn. Remember these pictures have the power to shape their ideas on how to dress and what their bodies should look like. I have gone into detail on these topics under the chapters "Body Image" and "Modesty and Makeup."

We must be mindful when purchasing any type of magazines for our children. They can be easily influenced by what the world would deem "harmless." As parents, we can't turn a blind eye when it comes to our children's hearts.

## 9.  No TV in Rooms

After a sleepover with one of her good friends, DeLaney came home absolutely exhausted because she didn't sleep well. Her friend had a TV in her room and she slept with it on all night long. She was addicted to the noise of the television and it made her feel safe hearing voices throughout the night. Although her friend thought she was resting well, she was actually not getting the proper sleep she needed with the extra light and noise in the room. She also had the ability to watch any show she wanted 24/7.

It is foolish for our children to have unmonitored access to TVs in their rooms. Why give the enemy extra ammunition to hijack our children's hearts? Our children's bedrooms should be a place of solace, rejuvenation, and creativity. Not placing a TV in our children's rooms is a great way to assist us in filtering the filth wanting to rush into their hearts.

## 10. Cell Phones

Technology has certainly come a long way from when I was a kid. I remember stretching the long, winding telephone cord from the kitchen around the corner to the living room, hoping to find a little bit of privacy from my family as I talked to my friends. Years later the heavy brick-like cell phones were birthed as we watched the elite of society indulge in this new form of communication. Who would have known this phone would evolve into a simple-to-use, handheld computer allowing access to the entire world? Not only did it make its way to the rich and poor but also into the hands of our children. Piggybacking off this technological wonder are social media apps that have become an integral part of modern culture.

Kevin and I waited longer than most parents to give our children a phone. Had it not been for some of their teachers in middle school asking them to take photos of assignments on the boards and to utilize the Internet for some of their in-class homework, we would have waited to give them a phone until high school. Just as we would never hand our children a cocked and loaded gun to play with, we have a responsibility as parents to provide the proper guidelines and accountability when allowing our children use of a cell phone. Without significant oversight, these devices have the potential to destroy our children's souls. We should be extremely vigilant about monitoring what they see, hear and who they interact with on their phone.

1 Peter 5:8 (NLT) says, "Stay alert! Watch out for your great enemy, the devil. He prowls around like a roaring lion, looking for someone to devour." Satan is always looking for open doors to get into our homes. Unfortunately, cell phones can be a huge gateway to invite all types of destructive activity into our children's lives. Setting boundaries and standing firm—in the face of our children's disapproval—will create an iron-clad barrier of defense against the enemy.

## 11. Filtering Music and Media

We are not purporting to boycott all media and music because there are some good choices out there. Thankfully, we have some trusted resources that can help us determine if our media or music choices are worth the watch or listen, and help us filter out the negative elements:

*Plugged In*—We have used Focus on the Family's Plugged In website for many years. They are an entertainment guide full of the reviews we need to make wise personal and family-friendly decisions about movies, videos, music, games, and books (www.pluggedin.com). We use this site quite extensively for movies. It is very simple to enter the name of the movie and view the complete summary of the movie. Every account of crude and profane language is noted along with spiritual elements, and sexual, violence, and drug and alcohol content.

This website has been an extraordinary tool in helping us make wise decisions on what we should allow our children to see and hear. Our children will verify that EVERY movie they want to see will first be researched on this website. Did our kids enjoy this process? Usually, no. We used this time as a teaching moment and for the benefits of guarding our hearts. On many occasions they were not allowed to attend a certain movie with friends. We were not popular parents and our kids weren't always happy with us. Now that they are in high school, they research it themselves and automatically know if they can see it or not. Kevin and I use this resource for our own viewing decisions. Guarding our heart doesn't come with an age limit!

*Netflix*—We cut off cable television about eight years ago and haven't missed it. With the high monthly fee, we were almost bound to watch TV to justify the cost. The commercials were getting racier and more sexually explicit, and we didn't want to deal with it anymore. Our subscription to Netflix allows us to choose the type of programming we want to watch, commercial-free. It also has a filter mechanism to set parameters on parental ratings allowed to view (www.netflix.com).

*VidAngel*—For Netflix or Amazon Prime users, many movies can be customized through VidAngel based on our personal choices, to filter out profanity, nudity, sexual content, and graphic violence (www.vidangel.com). It does require a monthly membership fee but it's worth it!

*TVGuardian*—TVG detects and mutes foul language on TV shows and DVD's by monitoring the hidden closed-captioning signal (www.tvguardian.com). When an offensive word is detected it mutes the sound from the sentence. Think about how much profanity we hear in a lifetime, especially from in-home movies and television shows. TVG can help filter out much of the foul language coming through our television sets.

*Lyric searches*—A quick Google search is all it takes to pull up the lyrics to any song. If we find our child listening to a song that doesn't fit our spiritual guidelines, we can use it as a moment to educate and not criticize. I remember the shocked faces of my children as I explained what the innuendos were in some of the songs on the radio. They immediately understood why the material was not heart-worthy.

## 12. Filtering Cell Phones

Limits and permissions can be set for any phone number on our account through our cell phone provider. By going into the profile area, we have the ability to block the following: Any adult content (pornography), certain Internet searches, malware, texts (sending and receiving), pictures and videos (sending and receiving), use of data, downloading and purchase of apps, voice calls (in and out), and specific numbers from being called or received.

## 13. Filtering the Internet

*Covenant Eyes* (CE) is an internet accountability service designed to monitor Internet activity including pornography on all of our internet browsers. CE sends a report to an accountability partner for our online choices. This software goes beyond just covering Internet activity by extending its protection to social media and other data-using apps (www. covenanteyes.com).

### 14. Family Locator

*Life360* is a one-stop shop to keep up with everyone in our family. It is based on a GPS tracking service and its benefits are numerous: keep up with everyone's current location, receive automated arrival updates, send automatic crash detection and emergency response services, and receive weekly driver reports (www.life360.com)

## Drinking Alcohol

Christians have differing opinions about the subject of alcohol. Kevin and I made the decision not to drink alcohol and to instruct our children in this way. It is not a heaven or hell issue, but it can be a life or death issue. Drunk driving is a nationwide problem and most of those who kill people on the roads made a bad choice to drink excessively. Some of those are teenagers and young adults who sadly underestimated the debilitating effects of the "harmless" drinks they consumed. Drinking alcohol was a staple with many on my father's side of the family. I have an abundance of childhood stories of relatives engaging in angered brawls, tear-filled soliloquies, and embarrassing stumbles and falls—all fueled by alcohol. Some relatives passed away from cirrhosis of the liver after succumbing to a lifetime of liquor. For Kevin and me, the risks of drinking alcohol outweighed any benefits whether it was taste, a calming effect, or the sense of acceptance and camaraderie in social settings.

We have taught our children that it usually won't offend someone to not drink but there is a high possibility that someone may be offended if we do, especially if we are church leaders.

*Since you are free to do as you please, be careful that this does not hurt a weak Christian. A Christian who is weak may see you eat food in a place where it has been given as a gift to false gods in worship. Since he sees you eat it, he will eat it also. You may make the weak Christian fall into sin by what you have done. Remember, he is a Christian brother for whom Christ died. When you sin against a weak Christian by making him do what is wrong, you sin against Christ. So then, if eating meat makes my Christian brother trip and fall, I will never eat it again. I do not want to make my Christian brother sin.*

—1 Corinthians 8:9-13 (NLV)

Our family has decided to abstain from drinking alcohol to protect our witness for Christ. As we mature as believers our choices must reach beyond ourselves. As we grow spiritually our decisions must be based on what's best for the entire body of Christ and not just our own desires. Guarding our hearts is extremely important but if we can help guard the heart of another from potential offense by not consuming alcohol, why not do so?

No one takes their first drink to become an alcoholic. Why risk it? No one goes out on the road after consuming alcohol to take another person's life. Why risk it? Why take the risk of possibly hindering a fellow brother or sister in Christ's spiritual walk? For our family, drinking is not worth it.

## Be Led by the Holy Spirit

Being led by the Holy Spirit is one of the best filtering mechanisms available to us as parents. God is faithful to reveal hidden things we need to know by His Spirit. Kevin and I have been prompted numerous times to scroll through our children's phones unannounced. Some of those checks have been very timely and we were able to ward off some potential catastrophes in the making. Our kids soon learned that God would call them out and it wasn't worth the hassle to attempt sneaking around!

If we get a check in our heart, or a sense that something just isn't right about a particular television show, it's best to switch to another TV program. If we don't have a green light with a particular movie, then we shouldn't allow our children to go see the movie. If we feel we've made a mistake in bringing our child to see a particular film, we shouldn't be afraid to walk out of the theater. We have a responsibility when we realize it's not something that would be edifying to us and our children to leave, regardless of whether we paid good money for the movie or not. If our children happen to be watching something at home with a group of friends that is beyond our boundaries, we shouldn't hesitate to change the channel or shut the TV off completely.

I'm reminded of an instance where a group of college friends had gathered at my husband's parent's house to watch the movie LaBamba. Kevin's dad happened to walk through the living room during a scene when an unmarried couple was having sex. Dad Schafer walked right over to the television set and turned it off. He said, "I'll have none of this LaBamba crud in my house!" We all sat there in awkward silence, looking at one another, wondering "What just happened?" This is a story none of us has forgotten and we bring it up often. Dad Schafer cared more about our hearts than the risk of embarrassing Kevin in front of all of his friends. Many of the people there mentioned later that they honored Kevin's father for taking a stand. We all agreed he did the right thing.

We must be sensitive when staying with family members with older teens or young adults. Instead of going to bed and allowing our child to stay up late with the older teens to watch whatever they may deem appropriate, or possibly play video games with mature content, it may be best to have them go to bed when we do. It may not be a popular move from our children's perspective, but it will definitely prevent them from being subjected to bad language or content. If the television is on during the day with questionable content, it is okay for us to kindly ask if we can watch something as a group that would be more appropriate for children. If the consensus wants to leave the show on, then we have a responsibility to move our children to another room and do something else with them.

Along these same lines, we must be watchful of our younger children hanging around with older kids. Although there is not a huge difference in age between a middle schooler and a high schooler, there is usually a level of maturity that is different. I've witnessed where middle schoolers had friends in high school and the parents allowed them to go to the movies and drive around with them like they were sixteen or seventeen years old. They may be exposed to certain conversations and scenarios that they are not prepared to handle. Also, they may begin to expect certain freedoms that they are not ready to receive. In general, it is best to pray for age-appropriate friends for our children and allow them to naturally progress in maturity within those relationships.

The Holy Spirit may deal with us about our child reading a particular book (possibly school-required ones) or seeing a certain play on a school field trip. He will guide us on how best to guard and protect our child's heart. We will cover more about this in the next section on "Sensitivity to the Holy Spirit."

On a side note, we never want to come off as condescending to other parents who may allow their children to see or do things that go against what we allow our children to see or do. Kevin and I instructed our children to call us to come and get them if they found themselves in a situation where the group was watching or doing something they know is not permissible. We encouraged them not to make a scene but just to say, "The movie goes against our family guidelines, but you don't have to turn it off for me. My parents are coming to get me." We should train our children to handle interactions with others with care and love when it comes to media boundaries. They must be mindful to never come off as superior or super spiritual because they do or don't watch something.

1 Corinthians 10:23 (NLT) says, "You say, "I am allowed to do anything"—but not everything is good for you. You say, "I am allowed to do anything"—but not everything is beneficial." When filtering media for our children we should ask ourselves: Is this really beneficial to my child's life or the state of their heart? How much junk will they have to sift through in order to receive the positive message of this show? Is this the type of image I want stored in my child's mind? Is this really something I should be watching since my child is watching me? Isn't my heart worth guarding, too?

All of the negative elements—profanity, sexual images, or violence—divide our children's hearts and contribute to the carnality within them. The flesh shouts, but the Holy Spirit whispers. As their hearts are opened to negative material, it will place our children at a disadvantage in clearly hearing God's voice and operating with confidence in the arena of faith. My pastor, Keith Cistrunk, says, "Whatever you feed on, feeds on you." God will still be able to use our children, but their effectiveness will be hindered. Our goal is not to have naive children but to guard their God-given innocence and purity.

God has set before us the ability to choose life or death (Deuteronomy 30:19). We should always choose life-giving material and we'll never go wrong! A great measuring rod is Philippians 4:8 (NIV), " Finally, brothers and sisters, whatever is true, whatever is noble, whatever is right, whatever is pure, whatever is lovely, whatever is admirable—if anything is excellent or praiseworthy—think about such things."

Guarding our children's hearts is no joke! In order for them to protect their spiritual edge and sharpness, it is a daily discipline. As we allow God to groom their spirit man, the clarity and focus they will receive will allow them, like an arrow, to pierce through their destinies with pinpoint accuracy.

## Sensitivity to the Holy Spirit

The world watched in horror on September 11, 2001 as our nation sustained one of the most violent terrorist attacks we had ever known. Catching everyone by surprise, a Boeing 767 struck the North Tower of the World Trade Center leaving behind a fiery trail of mass destruction. Many who witnessed the deadly collision from the South Tower began a swift exit down the elevators and stairwells. An announcement was made that the South Tower was secure, and it was safe to return to their offices. Some accounts say that at least one third to one half of the people headed back up the stairs to their offices, although many decided to continue their descent and safely got out of the building. No one could have predicted that within minutes another Boeing 767 would tear through the walls of the South Tower, leaving in its wake the death of thousands of innocent people.

On April 16, 2014, a South Korean ferry carrying 476 people—mostly students from a local high school on a field trip—sunk from an overloaded cargo hold. A video from the phone of a teenager who perished showed several students in his room nervously talking and laughing. The ship had begun to lean further and further to the point where they could not stand erect. Announcement after announcement was heard over the intercom instructing the students to remain in their cabins. Only those who disregarded the orders to stay in their rooms managed to make it to the ship's bridge, and were saved. Over 300 people died, most of them students trapped within the walls of their cabins.

In both of these tragic circumstances, incorrect instructions meant to keep people protected actually contributed to their demise. Many who had a feeling of urgency to leave the "safety" of their offices or cabins—resisting the guidance of well-meaning authorities—were saved.

Psalm 91:16 (NKJV) says, "With long life I will satisfy him, and show him My salvation." God has promised us long life and will warn us about anything that could take us or our children out early. He will clue us in to any imminent dangers that may be coming our way, and provide escape routes to bypass perilous situations. God was clearly speaking during the chaos on September 11 and on the ill-fated journey of the South Korean ferry. Unfortunately, some refused to dial in to what He was saying and they lost their lives.

Many times bad things have happened to us and we've responded with any of the following statements: "I knew I wasn't supposed to go there." "I had a feeling that something was going to happen." "I knew I should have been paying better attention." "I was speeding and I knew I needed to slow down." "I had a hunch I shouldn't have been with that person." We minimize these thoughts as "just me" or coincidental, instead of recognizing them as God speaking to us. His words are whispered and simple, and at times we can discount them as not being spiritual enough to be God. Our children need to be aware that in the busyness of life, it is tempting to be schedule-led and not Spirit-led. If they are willing to deviate from their normal plans, many untold tragedies and losses can be prevented. Multitudes of people would be alive today if they would have heeded the gentle nudges from the Holy Spirit. Obeying a random thought like "I should pull in and get some gas" or "a caramel mocha frappuccino sounds good right about now" could have yielded a few precious split seconds to divert them out of the pathway of a drunk driver, or being struck by a lethal brick thrown from an overhead bridge.

We may ask why did "this" bad thing happen? Why didn't God protect me or my child? Sadly, the reality is that many times God had provided a way of escape for us, but we were not paying attention to His instruction. Although God receives people into Heaven from a tragic accident or disease, it does not mean He takes them. We need not be fearful of the devil but understand that every day of our children's lives, he will try to bring about choreographed setups to take them out either physically or get them offtrack of their destinies. 1 Peter 5:8 (NKJV) says, "Be sober, be vigilant; because your adversary the devil walks about like a roaring lion, seeking whom he may devour."

As parents, we must be serious and watchful for these sudden attacks against our children. When we allow ourselves to be receptive to the Holy Spirit, we can instantly begin to respond in prayer to counteract evil strategies trying to be formed against them. The Holy Spirit may bring about a simple thought or a troubling dream concerning our children's welfare. Instead of allowing fear and worry to creep in, that is our time to jump into action and pray.

Just last year, I was driving down the road and the thought popped into my mind to pray for my son's safety. I didn't feel fearful about it, but I immediately said a simple prayer like "Lord,

I pray for Austin's protection. Give your angels special charge round about him and keep him in all of his ways." That was it. There was no fanfare or travailing in the Spirit. I kept driving and didn't think about it again. A couple of hours later, my husband called and said that a high-speed police chase had ensued down the street by our auto repair shop, and the man who was running from the police crashed his truck into the fence and main driveway of our building. Just a few minutes before the accident happened, Austin—who had been working at the shop—exited from that driveway. Did God divert our son from possible harm? Absolutely! Being sensitive to the Holy Spirit that day very well may have spared our son's life.

There are many excellent scriptures concerning God's promises for protection. God will certainly give his angels charge (Psalm 91) over our children, but part of His protection could be warning us or our children to not go somewhere, or to not do something. For example, let's say our child is invited to a sleepover and for whatever reason it doesn't set right in our hearts. Way down on the inside we don't feel like our child needs to go. We have an opportunity to respond to that check in our heart instead of making a blanket confession of, "Oh, they'll be alright. God will keep them safe." We can't override the leading of the Holy Spirit with a scripture confession. He is fervently broadcasting the right direction for us and our children's lives, but it is our responsibility to intercept His instructions and carry them out.

We see the dire consequences of not listening to God's voice,

> *But since you refuse to listen when I call and no one pays attention when I stretch out my hand, since you disregard all my advice and do not accept my rebuke, I in turn will laugh when disaster strikes you; I will mock when calamity overtakes you— when calamity overtakes you like a storm, when disaster sweeps over you like a whirlwind, when distress and trouble overwhelm you.*

—Proverbs 1:24-27 (NIV)

Our foolish rejection of the Lord's guidance ties His hands from being able to offer His protection and opens us up to the destructive plans of the enemy. Some of us hold God accountable for our tragedies when all along, He was the one wildly waving His arms that a bridge was out ahead. Choosing to recklessly proceed was our decision, in spite of our Father's passionate pleas to stop and turn around.

Listening to the Holy Spirit's guidance is not mysterious and hit-and-miss. Our children have a sensitivity to the voice of God and we need to help them recognize when God is talking to them. In 1 Samuel 3, God calls to young Samuel in the night and he did not realize who it was. Samuel's mentor and father figure, Eli the high priest, pointed out that God was speaking to Samuel and simply told him to make himself available to the instructions of the Lord. This is also our role as parents. We should ask our children some of the following questions:

"Have you prayed about this?" "What is God saying to you?" "How is He leading you?" "How does your spirit feel?" "Does it feel scratchy inside or do you have a sick feeling?" "Do you feel rushed or pressured to make this decision?" "Do you feel good inside about your choice?" "Do you feel peaceful and at rest in your heart?" We must teach our children to listen to the inner witness of the Holy Spirit and not make quick decisions based on human reasoning. What may seem like an obvious choice may not be the right one. Once our children get older we can be a sounding board for them, but we can't make every decision for them. I've seen God lead my children to do things I may have chosen to do differently. I realized that if I would have insisted on my own thoughts, I may have temporarily stalled the momentum towards their God-given course. It is not always easy, but we must trust God to lead our children. What a joy it is to know they can hear God's voice just like we do!

Because children are sensitive to the voice of God, we must be mindful to trust their intuition about certain matters. This is especially true in cases when adults ask our children to give them a hug or a kiss. I have witnessed time and again parents pressuring their children to hug or kiss a person, when their child obviously has no interest in doing so. I've heard parents scold their children for such reluctance as if they were doing a very bad thing. Kids sometimes have a sense about people before adults do. How many times have we heard about the seemingly normal friend of the family who sexually molested one of the children? If our children are not comfortable with hugging a certain individual, then allow them to shake their hand. As adults, we should also be mindful not to press other children to give us a hug or kiss. These outward physical expressions should be the choice of the child. I may be ridiculed for this, but I also feel the same way about making our children sit on Santa's lap just for the sake of having a holiday keepsake photo. We've all seen pictures of kids who are in a state of trauma on Santa's lap—bawling their heads off and looking at their parents like "why is this scary guy holding me, and why are you forcing me to stay with him?" Training our children that they must automatically respond to the physical requests from adults could be setting them up for a dangerous scenario.

It is unfortunate, but not everyone (including our own family members) has our child's best interest ats heart. For example, let's say a long-lost cousin calls to say he is going to be in town for the week on a job assignment and wants to stay at our house. We really don't know him, but he is a family member and we do recall playing with him a couple of times as a child at family reunions. Because he is "family," we may mindlessly say "yes" and give him the empty bedroom upstairs right next to our teenage daughter's bedroom. Another scenario could be that our aunt and uncle, who live on a farm, have invited our children to stay for a couple of weeks in the summer. Before giving an instant "yes," we should get the mind of the Lord on it. Although our aunt and uncle would probably do them no harm, what about the person who works on the farm that we don't know? What about the older cousin who drives recklessly (unbeknownst to our uncle and aunt) and would be taking our kids to get ice cream? God knows all of these possibilities and any potential destruction our children could encounter. When it comes to the welfare and safety of our children, we must be keenly aware of what God is saying, even when family members are involved.

Kevin and I have instructed our children that if they are in a life or death situation and the Holy Spirit tells them to do something contradictory to what their authority is saying, they have our permission to override the authority's directives. As we covered in the beginning of the chapter, those who did not heed the instructions of authority, and went with their gut instinct to get out of the South Tower or head to the boat deck from the sinking ferry, were saved. We have also advised our children to immediately tell us if anyone threatens to kill them or their family members in order to try and abuse them. This is a common tactic from abusers who use fear as a form of control. We don't want to invoke fear in our children about these things, but we want them to be aware of what our expectations are in those situations.

In Proverbs 1:33 (NIV) we see that heeding the voice of the Spirit of God brings great reward. It says, "But whoever listens to me will live in safety and be at ease, without fear of harm." God's protection is sure for our children. They are not sitting ducks waiting for tragedy to strike them. They are neither helpless nor defenseless against the surprise attacks of the enemy to steal from them, kill them, or destroy them (John 10:10). As parents, we should pray for our children to be at the right place, at the right time, with the right people. According to Proverbs 3:5-6 (NKJV) we can ask the Lord to direct our children's paths as they acknowledge and trust Him with all their hearts and not rely on their own understanding.

Sensitivity to the Holy Spirit strategically places our children in winning positions by bringing them supernatural insight and direction. When they are comfortable in hearing God's voice, our arrows will have the cutting edge to masterfully glide to exactly where they need to be.

## Confiding in Children

I had painstakingly saved up my money to purchase the "High Energy" record by K-tel. It contained some of the greatest hits of 1978, including Blondie's "Heart of Glass" and Gloria Gaynor's "I Will Survive." I watched eagerly as the daily TV commercials for the record popped on. I was only a few dollars away from hours of endless dancing in my room to my favorite songs! For a nine-year-old, this purchase was the biggest priority in the world. My parents were hosting a group of business professionals at our farm the monumental day I secured the rest of the funds needed for this treasured record. I sprinted outside and made my way to my mom. Although short of breath, I was able to speak out that I had the money in hand and asked if we could go and buy the record that evening. Of course, she said "Yes!" One of the gentleman standing by my mother, beamed as he listened to my excited plea and said to my mom, "Wouldn't it be so nice if buying a record was the only thing we had to worry about?" In my naivete, I was puzzled by his comment. I thought, "What else could be more important than this record?" My young perspective made me blissfully unaware of the daily rigors of responsibility in the adult world.

A couple of years after purchasing the record, things started getting tumultuous within my parent's marriage and farming business. Although they were only operating in the amount of knowledge they knew at the time, they began to reveal to me certain indiscretions within their relationship, the serious financial state of our business, as well as details of failed transactions with their business partners. Using me as a sounding board placed me in a precarious position of constant worry about our future, while feeling completely helpless to offer any type of assistance or productive input.

Children don't have the experience or the wherewithal to process many of the challenges we encounter as adults. As parents, we must be very mindful not to needlessly and prematurely shatter their tender mindsets by confiding in them about mature issues beyond their control. Childhood is a special gift from God that contains a fragility and innocence worth protecting.

My pastor, Brett Jones, wisely instructs us to seek counsel from those who are winning in the areas we are lacking. For example, we probably should not be seeking marriage advice from someone who has had five failed marriages. Along those same lines, what benefit or advice would we expect to receive from our children by disclosing our problems to them? Are they going to help us come up with a strategy to get caught up on our mortgage payments? Will they give us recommendations on how to grow our struggling marriages or other relationships? Do they have the skill to look at our budgets and see where we can cut corners? No! Just because our kids are easy targets for mindlessly venting our frustrations, we should think before we blast them with our negativity. Proverbs 29:11 (**DARBY**) says, "A fool uttereth all his mind; but a wise [man] keepeth it back." If we are listening, the Holy Spirit will arrest us before we divulge something we shouldn't to our children. We should confide in a spiritually mature adult who can actually pray with us, support us, and encourage us through our times of crisis. To the best of our ability, allow our kids to be kids and enjoy the fleeting time of having less responsibilities in life.

If money is tight and our children are asking for something that we don't have the funds for, instead of giving them a blow- by-blow of all the bills we currently have and saying, "Why would you even ask for something like that? You know we can't afford that." Why not say, "Right now it's not in the budget but if it's something you really desire, let's ask God to make a way for you to have it." God is ultimately our children's provider, and Kevin and I have watched Him supply things for our children that were totally out of the scope of what our income would have allowed for us to buy them. We could have easily missed those miraculous moments if we had not adjusted our children's focus from our present financial status to God's supernatural ability.

Burdening our children with undue pressure about things currently going wrong in our world will only bog them down. Utilizing trusted and mature believers to help us through challenging times will not only sharpen us as parents but will also protect our arrows from the dulling impact of using them as our little confidants.

## Don't Uncover Your Children

I listened intently while on the other end of the phone my friend revealed her frustration with her son and his failing grades. "I don't understand what the problem is. I am so upset with him right now and he had better get his act together!" she exclaimed. In the background, I faintly heard her son's voice talking to his younger sibling. I immediately asked, "Is your son in the room right now?" She said, "Yes. Why do you ask?" I said, "Because he probably wouldn't appreciate you sharing this with me, and is most likely embarrassed hearing you tell me about his bad grades. Why don't we talk at another time when he's not there, and I can offer my advice then?"

On another occasion, I watched a mother share—as a comical icebreaker in front of a group of people—some of her young son's idiosyncrasies. Unfortunately, the son was there and I personally witnessed his little face sink with humiliation as the room erupted with laughter.

We must put ourselves in our children's shoes and think how humiliating it would be for everyone to know our "dirty laundry." It is our parental responsibility to make sure to guard our children's trust by not uncovering their transgressions with other people. We should use discretion and only reveal things when absolutely necessary, whether with family or close friends. Kevin and I have made a point to respect our children in this way. We are also very cautious not to compare our children to other children or their siblings, especially in an unfavorable light. Most of our children's negative behaviors are temporary and can be rectified by proper discipline and training. If our children are having difficulties, there is nothing beneficial in being transparent with a lot of people about their challenges. If we need some special guidance, we should go to someone who has proven success in parenting. If we have questions about our teenager, we should speak with someone who has raised world-changing teenagers, not someone who has only a toddler or no children at all!

We should also keep in mind that social media should not be a platform to vent, journal, or receive instructional consensus regarding crucial life and family issues. In times of distress and when emotions are running high, it can be easy to quickly put out a thought or post a picture without thinking it through. We must also be watchful in making fun of something our children did or said on social media because this can be a great source of embarrassment to them. Before posting anything of that nature, it would probably be best to get our children's permission. When it comes to our spouse, we should use the same guidelines.

Posting a prayer request of our children's personal trials on social media may not be the wisest choice. It is not the quantity of prayers that turns the ear of God but the faith behind the prayers. Although many people say "I'm praying for you," we can never be sure that they really are. If they are praying, they may not even be sure how to pray and may possibly be praying in opposition to what really needs to happen. Some people are just glad they scrolled to our post and now have an interesting tidbit about our child. We should reveal any prayer needs or glean spiritual direction from a select group of trusted individuals in a private setting. When we uncover our children to the multitudes, it has the potential to hurt them.

Proverbs 17:9 (NIV) says, "Whoever would foster love covers over an offense, but whoever repeats the matter separates close friends." When our children know we have their backs and are diligently protecting their dignity, the security it brings gives them a laser sharp edge to break through any temporary barriers they may encounter.

## No Gossip or Bashing

It was the fall of 1994, and Kevin and I were living in Tulsa while he was attending Rhema Bible College. We were faithful members of the local church connected with the college which allowed us to meet several wonderful couples in the young married class. We invited a few of them to our home one night for fun, food, and fellowship. After the meal, we all sat in the living room exchanging stories and lots of laughs. Somehow the conversation took a turn and one of our friends began to discuss his complaints about the senior pastor of our church. The atmosphere in the room became awkward and it was obvious that the other people there were not comfortable with what was being said. Doing our best to bring the discussion around to another topic, the gentleman would not budge from his soap box. A righteous indignation rose up from within me and I stood to my feet. Before I could even think my words leapt out, "We do not talk about our ministry leadership like that in our home, and we are going to have to ask you and your wife to leave." The guy raised his eyebrows in disbelief and said, "Are you serious?" I said, "I am very serious" as I walked to the front door and opened it. They sheepishly scurried out the door and were never invited back to our home again.

Thankfully even as a young married couple, Kevin and I knew gossip was an open door to destruction. 1 Corinthians 12:12-14 (NLT) says, "The human body has many parts, but the many parts make up one whole body. So it is with the body of Christ . . . ." Because we are the body of Christ, we have a responsibility to treat each one of the members with respect and honor. In 1 Corinthians 11:29-31 (ERV) we see how detrimental it can be when we don't highly esteem our brothers and sisters in Christ. This passage says in respect to the Lord's communion, "If you eat and drink without paying attention to those who are the Lord's body, your eating and drinking will cause you to be judged guilty. That is why many in your group are sick and weak, and many have died. But if we judged ourselves in the right way, then God would not judge us." Being insensitive to the other members of the body of Christ can be a catalyst for prolonged illness and premature death.

Our ultimate guidelines for life come from Mark 12:30-31 (ERV), "Love the Lord your God with all your heart, all your soul, all your mind, and your strength. The second most important command is this: Love your neighbor the same as you love yourself . . . ."

God places a high priority on loving Him and loving others. It is important to raise our children to treat others the way they would want to be treated and to operate according to God's love. 1 Corinthians 13:7 (AMPC) says, "Love bears up under anything and everything that comes, is ever ready to believe the best of every person . . . ." With love as their guide, our children can learn to be respectful of other people. Unless there are matters of abuse or they are at severe odds with either a coach, teacher, pastor, or youth pastor (and in need of intervention), children should never speak ill of another person.

Kevin and I do our best to place a positive spin on a situation if our kids start talking about someone in a disparaging manner. A great way to do this is to empathize with their frustration by saying something like, "I understand the way you are feeling, but let's try looking at it from a different angle. Maybe they have had a bad day. Maybe things aren't going well at home and they are hurt. A lot of times, hurt people will hurt people." We can point our children back to Jesus in times like these and ask Him for His perspective. We should always lead them to pray for the person who has wronged them. It's amazing to witness a negative conversation come full circle by having our children bless a person who has hurt them, and bless the Heavenly Father who can ultimately bring about true reconciliation.

We live in a society that thrives on criticism. With social media, we are one click away from commenting about what we like and don't like. We love to express our opinions on who the next superstar musician will be, who has the most creative cupcakes, and who wore the best dress to the Oscars. Saying how we feel about anything under the sun has become an acceptable form of entertainment. If we are not careful, we can carry this scrutinizing evaluation and inspection into our homes where judgment becomes a normal part of our family culture. We may be swimming upstream on this one, but we must create a "no bashing" zone in our homes. No bashing would include our family members, our ministry leaders, our spouses, our children and their siblings. Oh, and let's not forget our president. Many people in our country feel they have a license to harshly criticize our president. However, nowhere in scripture does it say, "judge those who are in rule," but it does say to pray for them (1 Timothy 2:1-2).

As easily as we can train our children to disrespect people by focusing on their shortcomings, we can just as easily help them to view others through the filter of God's love. Proverbs 19:11 (AMPC) states, "Good sense makes a man restrain his anger, and it is his glory to overlook a transgression or an offense." It takes no discipline whatsoever to mock someone or point out something they have done wrong. But it is to a man's or woman's glory when they choose to focus on the good in a person.

It is very tempting to gossip and speak negatively about leadership or coworkers on the job. When Austin began a summer internship with a large company, we strongly admonished him in this area. We shared that if someone would talk to him about others, they would talk to others about him. Our children can never go wrong when they choose to build bridges instead of walls and treat everyone, especially their supervisors, with honor, respect, and dignity. Though it may be uncomfortable to not give in to the pressures of gossip, in the long run others will respect our children and know they can be trusted.

Children are very impressionable. I have seen teenagers and young adults who vehemently oppose Christianity because of parents who did not use discretion when speaking about other Christians, especially ministry leaders. On Sundays after church, many dining room tables contain a delicious hot meal including roast pastor. If we habitually portray that our circle of ministry leadership is off base, unfair, out of love, and unscriptural, then our children may receive a skewed sense that Christianity is a big scam. Our judgmental conversations can plant offense in the hearts of our children. Mark 4:17 (AMPC) outlines that when offense takes root it steals the Word that has been sown and can cause someone to fall away from Jesus. The Bible says that people will know we are Christians by how we love the brethren (John 13:35). It is easy to love those who are lovable. We must show our children how it is to love those who may not be easy to love at certain times, which may include those in church leadership. We get into trouble when we place our pastors and ministry leaders on pedestals where they can do no wrong. They would be the first to tell us that they are not perfect and need much grace. We should shield our children as much as possible from ministry negativity. If we are experiencing relationship challenges, especially within the church, those things should be dealt with privately and scripturally. According to Matthew 18:15, if a brother offends us, we should go directly to that person and seek reconciliation.

I remember a story by my mentor, Brother Kenneth E. Hagin, Sr. He was eating with a group of other ministers and they began speaking negatively about an evangelist they all knew. Brother Hagin wasn't saying a word, but after a while the ministers asked him what he thought about the gentleman. He stopped eating, looked up from his plate, and said, "He has a nice head of hair." He then picked up his fork and began eating again. Brother Hagin was well aware of the potentially disastrous consequences of shredding a fellow brother in Christ with peers who should have known better.

1 Corinthians 16:14 (NLV) admonishes us, "Everything you do should be done in love." We can never go wrong when we steer our children to view and speak of others through the lens of God's love. Embracing the good in people and blessing those who may persecute them, will grind the edges off our arrows and sharpen them to accomplish their mission.

# ARROWS MUST BE TESTED

We can hold in our hands a finely crafted arrow, beautifully painted with pinstripes, bedazzled with rhinestones, and a finely chiseled, razor-sharp arrowhead. It is obvious that extreme effort has been taken to create every element of the arrow—from the shaft, to the balancing mechanism, to the arrowhead. No expense has been spared. To the naked eye, it looks like the most impressive and luxurious arrow in town. However, the reason for the arrow is not its appearance, but its performance as a fully functional and potentially destructive weapon. Its capability must be tested. Does it fit well within the bow? Does it fly smoothly through the air? Is it sharp enough to penetrate an object? The mechanics of the arrow must be examined and proven for it to optimally perform. This crucial feedback will allow every aspect of the arrow to be fine-tuned, enabling it to effectively carry out its purpose. In the heat of the battle, these important adjustments will make the difference between victory or defeat.

After years of investing in our children, it is our responsibility as parents to place a demand on the training they've received. How cruel it would be to put our eighteen-year-old out on the door step with absolutely no proving and say, "You're on your own. Good luck and our fingers are crossed! We hope you do okay." Under our watchful care and within the safety of our homes, there are things we can do to test and fine-tune our arrows to ensure they fly far and with accuracy.

## The Uncomfortable Child

Before baby eagles are born, the mother eagle prepares the nest with soft down from other animals. Underneath the down, she lines the nest with thorns, sharp rocks, and prickly branches. As the baby eagles grow and are ready to fly from the nest, the mother eagle begins to remove the down bit by bit until the baby eagles are so uncomfortable they have no choice but to leave. Is this harsh? No, it's healthy. The mother eagle understands the capability of her children before they even realize it.

As parents, it can hurt us to witness our children experiencing any type of discomfort. If there is something we can do to help remedy a situation, it is our natural inclination to rush in to make things better. Ironically, it isn't our responsibility to make our children comfortable. Taking a lesson from the mother eagle, uncomfortable situations can be excellent teaching moments for our children. These times help them mature into independent adults and push them to look to God as their resource and solution giver.

As an example, let's say our child left their homework or lunch at home and asked us to bring it to him or her. We have a choice right then and there to train our child that whenever something is left behind, we will not drop everything to get it into their hands. What I have done in these situations, is give my child a warning for that school year. I will tell them that if they leave their homework or lunch at home again, I won't be bringing it to them. They will have to face the consequences of either receiving a bad grade or being hungry for lunch. We've done the same thing concerning them getting up for school. Yes, we've let them miss a day of school because they overslept, but I think it took only one time. It's amazing how quickly they learn to listen for the alarm if they know we're not going to wake them up. Just think ahead to college. How miserable would it be to have to wake them up every day? We need to be sensitive to our children's earlier grade levels, but by middle school they need to be well on their way to making responsible decisions. We are setting our children up for failure if we program them that with any wrong choice we'll always sweep in and save the day.

It is important to include our children in decision-making processes. How will they ever learn if we make all of the decisions for them? When they're younger, we could pick two outfits for them and see which one they'd like to wear. We could give them a choice between a ham sandwich, or a peanut butter and jelly sandwich. As they get older and come to us for answers, we shouldn't immediately tell them what to do. One of my pastors, Keith Cistrunk, uses the phrase "put the 'on us' back on them." We must be cautious to not hand deliver answers to our children, allowing them to operate without any thought or creativity. The more resources we give our children, the less resourceful they can become. It is good to ask our children, "What do you think you should do?" "What do you think God is saying?" and ask further questions to hopefully draw out a correct solution that comes from them and not from us. We talk about this in detail in the section "Sensitivity to the Holy Spirit."

Some choices aren't a make-or-break and we can leave it up to the discretion of the child. Giving our children freedom to make decisions, without having to keep one eye on us at all times, is part of the process of growing up. I've witnessed adults who were hesitant and fearful to commit to a decision, because they were never trusted or encouraged by their parents to do so. We never want to cripple our children into believing they can't make a decision without us.

Many parents who pick their kids up from school have experienced the long car lines. Kids always prefer for us to be first in line, so they don't have to wait too long. Sometimes that requires being twenty minutes early before the final school bell rings. However, if we run into a snag in our schedule and we are a few minutes late to pick them up, they shouldn't experience an emotional meltdown. Kevin's dad used to say when they were children and complained, "Endure a little bit, will you?" Allowing patience to have its perfect work in our children is a good thing (James 1:4). This would include sharing toys with other children. Kevin and I had three stair-step children who were always vying for each other's toys. We ended up getting a kitchen timer and setting it for five minutes. Once the ringer went off, they had to pass the toy to their sibling. That's hard for a child and a few minutes seems like a lifetime to them. But when they stuck it out, they were rewarded and learned to wait patiently. Endurance-stretching opportunities are not comfortable, but they are seeding into our children's ability to successfully cope with adversity.

If one of our children is having difficulty in a certain school subject, we should have them speak to the teacher first instead of immediately contacting the teacher for our child. Again, this is especially true for older children in middle school or high school. We should coach our child about how to approach the conversation and what types of questions to ask. I have found that most teachers are very helpful when we open the lines of communication. They are not mind readers. They may not know that our child is having a problem understanding until they get a bad grade on a test. It may be difficult for our child to go and talk to a teacher because of embarrassment or fear, but it is an important lesson for them to learn. Asking questions and searching for understanding are lifelong habits that need to be developed. If a good game plan is not determined, then we may need to intervene. Ultimately, our children should be learning how to find their own solutions without our constant oversight.

I am reminded of a call I took in the Member Care department from a mother calling on behalf of her forty-year-old son who was having marriage problems. She asked about the details of our counseling process and wanted to know available appointment times for her son and daughter-in-law. The main question in my mind was "why was her son not making this phone call?" It didn't take Einstein to realize that the biggest problem this guy had probably wasn't his wife but his mother who was standing in the way of him progressing in maturity, and taking full responsibility as a husband. Genesis 2:24 says a man should leave his parents and cleave to his wife. It was obvious that his mother was still deeply involved in his life, to the point where she was taking charge of the welfare of his marriage. Somewhere along the way, she neglected or refused to equip her son with the necessary skills to deal with the challenges of life.

It feels good to be needed by our children. However, their need and dependence on the Lord should eventually surpass their need and dependence on us. God did not bless us with children just to give us warm fuzzies or to satisfy a void in our life. Do we enjoy our children, and have they enriched our lives? Of course! But we must be watchful to not place our children in a role they were never meant to fill. Some of us have experienced a massive amount of pain, and the greatest joy we have is in our children. However, this can yield unhealthy expectations as we unintentionally place extreme pressure on them to make us happy.

If we're not careful, we can begin idolizing our children, consumed with catering to their every whim. This creates an inordinate affection which is an overly obsessive love for something. Exodus 20:3 (ERV) says, "You must not worship any other gods except me." It seems almost unfathomable to worship our children more than God, but it can happen. If our whole world revolves around our children and their activities, and our actions show that nothing else matters but them, something is out of balance. Our smothering devotion can backfire when our children grow older and one of two things can happen: They will either distance themselves from us—possibly not even interacting with us at all—to loosen themselves from our stifling influence. Or, they may bypass moving to other parts of the country to fulfill Spirit-led career opportunities and dreams to avoid hurting us.

When our children are small they need a lot of time and attention, and much of life will be consumed with them. I always tell first-time parents that there is a great temptation to use our children as an excuse from serve opportunities, going to church, attending different events, etc. We must use wisdom when committing to things, as we have to keep our children's nap schedules and some of their activities in mind; however, we can easily hide behind our children and end up serving them, instead of them learning how to serve alongside us.

Chores are an excellent way of making children uncomfortable. They teach our children responsibility and give them a sense of satisfaction as they make a contribution to the family. When our son was about four-years-old, I made him a small chore chart that was on his bedroom door. Since he couldn't read,

I drew squares and pictures to help him know what was expected each morning. One picture was a toothbrush to remind him to brush his teeth. Another one was a picture of his bed to remind him to make his bed. Another picture was a comb to remind him to comb his hair. Another picture was a trash can to remind him to take out the trash in the bathroom. Each morning, he excitedly went to his chore chart to start marking his day off! We allowed our children at early ages to cook with us, and showed them how to properly use a knife. I'm not talking about giving a toddler a knife. When they are four or five years old, they can hold a small paring knife and learn to chop things if we school them on what to do. They will surprise us on what they are able to master with training. They don't know unless they are taught. It can be a challenge to slow down and gently guide our children, because we're usually rushing to make a meal. If we take the time, we are only going to expand their ability to help us! Our children have also laundered their own clothes since late elementary school. We showed them how, and what a blessing this has been to us.

As children age, of course, they will have more responsibilities. It is really up to each family to know what is to be expected from each child. But a sure sign of maturity is when our children start doing things they were not asked to do. I remember one summer day when Austin—who was in middle school at the time—decided to clean out the garage. It had become quite cluttered but with it being out of sight, it was mostly out of mind. When I asked him why he decided to tackle the garage, his reply was, "I wanted to help Dad out and surprise him." We can stretch our children by encouraging them to be proactive in life and do more than is expected. We should encourage our children to be reliable and always follow through with projects they've committed to. They should always be on time and in fact, be ten to fifteen minutes early to plan for delays. When our children's names come to mind, they should be known as faithful and extremely dependable. Those who are most successful, and usually rise to leadership positions, are the ones who always think a few steps ahead and complete the tasks they're given.

Going above and beyond can become a lifestyle for our children but it comes through small, daily choices, which many times are unpleasant to the flesh. For instance, when we go to the grocery store and see stray carts all around us as we're walking in, train our kids to grab a cart or two and roll them to the cart holding area. When we're walking in the parking lot, especially at church, pick up trash in our path and throw it away. We can show our children how to honor other people's establishments and although no one may know we helped pick up trash or put a cart away, God does. He looks at every self-sacrificing act as a deposit which he credits to our account. These little, consistent, honorable efforts will bring about unexpected harvests in our children's lives!

I once heard a story about a daughter who was complaining to her dad that her life was miserable, and she was sick and tired of dealing with problems. Her father took her to the kitchen and filled three pots of water and placed them on the stove. As the water began to boil, he placed a potato in one pot, an egg in the second pot, and coffee beans in the third pot. He then explained that the potato, egg, and coffee beans all faced the same adversity in the boiling water, but they all reacted differently. The potato went in strong, hard, and unrelenting but in the boiling water, it became soft and weak. The egg was fragile, with the thin outer shell protecting its liquid interior. When it was placed in the boiling water, it became hard. However, the ground coffee beans were unique. After they were exposed to the boiling water, they changed the water and created something new. He then asked his daughter, "Which one are you?" It is a guarantee that hard times will come for our children. John 16:33 (NIV) says, "I have told you these things, so that in me you may have peace. In this world you will have trouble. But take heart! I have overcome the world." When adversity comes, will our children bend under pressure or will they be able to flex while imparting a spirit of victory into the atmosphere? Allowing our children to make decisions, giving them more mature responsibilities, and permitting them to receive negative consequences from bad choices, are all things we can do to ensure their readiness for the adult world. These simple but effective tests are ways we can lovingly fine-tune and help our arrows become uncomfortable enough to make the adjustments necessary to soar.

## Interacting with Society

The long-awaited day for our daughter to receive her driver's permit had come. "What is her birthday?" the Texas DPS representative asked as she looked up at me from her computer. I focused my attention on my fifteen-year-old daughter and said, "Kamryn, go ahead and tell this nice lady what your birthday is." The attendant looked a little confused with my redirect, as it was obvious she was not accustomed to teenagers speaking on their own behalf. She did not realize the important training I was conducting at that moment. I was pushing Kamryn beyond her comfort zone to help her develop skills she would need for the rest of her life. This was one of many occasions used for her to practice interacting with people, especially strangers. As parents, we must look for moments for our child to speak and answer questions to the best of their ability. If we are at a restaurant—even when our children are three to four years old—we can ask our children to tell the waiter what they want to eat and drink. They probably won't like doing this at first because it is someone they don't know and it's easier to have mom or dad speak for them. As time goes by, they will become more accustomed to answering questions. For children and teenagers who are so painfully shy (they can't look anyone in the eye or hold a conversation) it may be that we've not pushed them to interact with people, or it possibly could be a spiritual situation. 2 Timothy 1:7 says, "God has not given us a spirit of fear but of power, love and a sound mind." If it seems that there is a spirit of oppression or fear that infiltrates our children's actions, we have authority through Christ Jesus to come against any demonic activity that would cause fear in our children. We can speak directly to the source and say "Satan, in the name of Jesus. I command any demonic activity or fearful spirits assigned to my child to cease and desist all operations against them now, in the name of Jesus. Amen."

Once our children are in middle school, they should be able to call in an order for a pizza. We can write everything down for them to say and gently guide them (if needed) while they are on the phone. How many hours will be spent in a lifetime with a customer service representative on the phone trying to get resolution? Ha! Our children have no idea! They might as well get used to having those types of conversations over the phone now.

When it comes to college entrance interviews, job interviews, and conversations with customers and colleagues, we can set our children up for success. Stretching them to think on their feet and speak for themselves are perfect ways to ensure our arrows will be ready to take on the world!

## Friends

Having friendships is an important part of growing up, and is a basic need in being a healthy adult. Not every child makes friends as easily as others. Maybe they aren't a social butterfly and are more introverted. Nevertheless, every child needs a friend. Quality overrules quantity any day. It's not important for our child to have tons of friends, but we should ask God for at least one. We should encourage our children to step out of their comfort zone and talk to potential friends. Proverbs 18:24 (JUB) says, "The man that has friends must show himself to be a friend . . . ." However, when they begin making connections with people, we have to be sensitive to not instantly shoot the relationship down. Some Christian parents shield their children from every child their age, because they are looking for the perfect kid to be their child's friend. As we know, perfect children don't exist! These type of parents foster a general distrust and fear within their children, and they start unconsciously shutting people out. Many times these isolated kids aren't able to relate to their peers, which as a Christian can be a problem—they stick out like a sore thumb and their discomfort around children their own age builds walls.

Whether Christian children go to public, private, or home school, they will assuredly have multiple ministry opportunities within their peer groups. Students these days are going through challenges, temptations, and pains that generations before us have never experienced. Never has there been a time so needed for our children to be a light. The Barna Group study confirms that ninety-four percent of adult Christians made their decision for Jesus prior to the age of eighteen. The harvest is ripe and our children, with proper guidelines, can become key players used by God to proclaim the message of Christ.

Kevin and I witnessed our children having different levels of friends. They attended public school and had both non-Christian and Christian acquaintances whom they may have shared a class or extracurricular activity—such as choir or theatre— with. These were more surface relationships where our kids showed God's love in action more than preaching about Him. Their main focus was planting seeds of kindness.

Another level of friendship was those whom they enjoyed enough to spend more time together. Not everyone was a Christian, but mainly these students were invited to our home for a meal and a wholesome movie. Under our guidance these kids were able to witness a family that laughs together, and loves, encourages, and sincerely cares about each other. We were able to ask questions about them and take a genuine interest in what was going on in their lives. We counted it as a time to be a witness for Christ and plant seeds of God's love. Many of our kids' friends especially enjoyed their interaction with Kevin, and he will be forever endeared by them as our "Kingwood Dad." (We are from Kingwood, TX.)

The last level of friendship was their close friends. Each one of our children had at least one friend who could offer them accountability and sharpen them as a believer in Christ Jesus. These types of friendships are the most important ones as they can impact the direction of our children's lives. We must be cautious to not pressure our children to make a certain person their "best friend." We have learned over the years, that these types of relationships happen organically and can't be forced. We also must understand that certain friendships may only be for a season and although we may be very fond of our child's friend, we have to be willing to flow with what relationships are most productive for our child at any given time.

We must be diligent to pray for our children concerning their friendships and support them in their endeavors (albeit sometimes challenging) to connect with those who will be a strong support system for them. Proverbs 13:20 (NLT) says, "Walk with the wise and become wise; associate with fools and get in trouble." Leaning on God's wisdom, our arrows' friendships will help them pass the test in moving beyond the bow to their divine destination.

## Budgets

In 2017 Ramsey Solutions, a leading company in financial education, conducted a study of more than 1,000 U.S. adults. This study showed that money fights are the second leading cause of divorce, behind infidelity. Many Americans are enslaved by the bondage of debt and their marriages are suffering the consequences. Cultivating a respect for money, and creating spending and saving guidelines for our children will most definitely impact the health of their future marriages. Dave Ramsey's Financial Peace University's program encourages the use of cash whenever possible, and using an envelope system to separate the budgeted cash into different expenditures such as grocery money, entertainment, personal spending money, etc.

When our children were in late elementary school, Kevin and I decided to incorporate this system for school shopping. We would give them a budget for clothes and school supplies, and put the allotted cash in an envelope. We would drive them to whichever stores they wanted to go, and they had the ability to buy their own school clothes, shoes, and supplies based on what they had in their envelope. We showed them how to look online for sites such as retailmenot.com for coupons, and explained how they could make the most out of their money. From that point on, school shopping was a breeze.

Once my children could drive, we allowed them to go shopping on their own. They all had pretty strong ideas on what was stylish and what was not. If they had a question about a purchase, they would text a picture for feedback. It was a better experience for them because they didn't have to keep telling me how much they didn't like the things I was picking out for them. It was a better experience for me because I didn't have to hear them telling me all the reasons they didn't like what I was choosing. It was a win/win! We've also given our children an envelope with money they could spend on school lunch supplies for the week. It was exciting for them to go to the store and pick out exactly what they wanted to eat!

When our children began driving, they had more opportunities for social gatherings. Before we knew it, they were asking for extra money to go to the movies, get coffee, go bowling, go out to eat, etc. Kevin and I sat our children down and celebrated that they were growing older and that wanting to do more was understandable. However, we declared we would no longer be a human ATM for them. We told them with age comes more responsibility and going forward, they would be responsible for their own gas and entertainment, including eating out with friends. Once the initial shock wore off, they realized we were serious. Because of their schedules, a steady job working at a fast food restaurant or grocery store would not work. We encouraged them to draw upon the creative power of God on the inside of them, and He would show them what to do. Our son began helping a lot at our auto repair shop and got involved in buying and selling vehicles. In fact, by the time he was eighteen years old, he had purchased three cars with cash. One of our daughters started a successful tutoring business, and both of our daughters did some babysitting. Each one had their own checking and savings accounts with a debit card, and learned how to keep a check on their balances. Some parents expect their children to buy their cars or car insurance. Whatever those things are, they will need to be clearly communicated to the children.

Teaching kids to responsibly handle money and stay within a budget perpetuates lifelong habits of effective money management. We want our children to be productive adults who are able to successfully support themselves. Getting their focus off of us as the one who meets their needs and on to the true Provider, will enhance their dependence and trust in God.

Deuteronomy 8:18 (**NKJV**) says "And you shall remember the Lord your God, for it is He who gives you power to get wealth . . . ." Our God longs to bless our children and show them ways of creating abundant provision in their lives. Our arrows will appreciate the testing received in this area as they confidently sail unhindered by the tempting traps of debt.

## Choosing Your Emotions

In Stephen Covey's *The 7 Habits of Highly Effective People*, he relays the story of Viktor Frankl. Mr. Frankl endured a torturous experience in one of the Jewish concentration camps during WWII. He ended up losing everyone in his family through the gas chamber, except for his sister. He was at the total mercy of the German soldiers. Although his time there was horrific, he realized there was one freedom that could never be taken away from him and that was how he would respond to his circumstances. Instead of giving up, he chose hope. He chose not to hate his captors. He chose to encourage and uplift his fellow prisoners. The guards may have had control over his body, but they could never seize control over his mind. As parents, we can teach our children along these lines. They have a responsibility or better said, a "response-ability" to choose how they will feel about things. Perhaps they may say "my sister made me angry" or "you made me angry" or "that made me angry." We can show them that nothing or no one can really make them do anything. They choose to be angry and since their anger is a choice, they can choose not to be angry. They can choose a peaceful response, though it may not come naturally.

In the book *Speaking the Truth in Love, How to be an Assertive Christian*, it says, "If you tie your emotional well-being to other people's behavior, you'll probably be upset a great deal of the time. Rarely will others dedicate their lives to behaving only in ways that are designed to make you happy. You must own your feelings and accept responsibility for modifying your feelings. If you can accept the fact that other people are not directly causing your emotional life, you can then give attention to your own thinking."

We can teach our children how to control their feelings and that they can choose to create their emotions. Proverbs 16:32 (NKJV) says, "He who is slow to anger is better than the mighty, and he who rules his spirit than he who takes a city." We are able to control our emotions through the help of the Holy Spirit. Galatians 5:22-23 (NKJV) reveals that the fruit of the Spirit within us is love, joy, peace, longsuffering, kindness, goodness, faithfulness, gentleness, and self-control. We can help our children develop a recognition of the Spirit of God within them, so they can draw upon those things that counteract the negativity they may be feeling. As our arrows are tested in the arena of their emotions, they will receive an enhanced ability to maneuver through challenging situations and reach their ultimate assignment.

## Healer in the House

Feeling the warm, familiar grip of my young husband's hand clasped around mine, we walked together into Loyola Medical Center in Chicago. It was the day after our first year anniversary, June 17, 1991 and definitely not the celebration we had envisioned. After a series of excruciating headaches and numbness in his face and limbs, Kevin had been diagnosed with hydrocephalus which is swelling on the brain. His brain fluid was not draining properly and was dangerously building up, threatening to cause permanent paralysis. The neurosurgeon would implant a shunt through his skull into his brain cavity which would allow the excess fluid to drain through a tube leading to his stomach. The surgery was successful and within a few weeks, Kevin was able to resume life as normal. He enjoyed three headache-free years but when an incapacitating headache came on suddenly, we knew we had to get him immediately to the hospital. Another shunt revision surgery followed and in the course of six months, he endured two additional shunt revision surgeries. The thought crossed our minds that this could possibly be our new normal. Because the doctors could not guarantee the length of time the shunt would work or how his body would receive the implant, they said we should be prepared for additional surgeries.

It was a sobering thought as we came to the conclusion that medical intervention could not offer us a permanent solution. We had prayed for God's help during the surgeries and for a favorable outcome, but we realized we would have to put our entire trust in Him for Kevin's healing. We began to seek God as never before and although we believed in the healing promises in the Bible, we allowed them to take deep root into our hearts. Kevin maximized his time of recovery by memorizing, meditating, and confessing

God's healing promises over his life. Proverbs 4:20-22 (NKJV) says, "My son, give attention to my words; Incline your ear to my sayings. Do not let them depart from your eyes; Keep them in the midst of your heart; For they are life to those who find them, and health to all their flesh."

Kevin's health was restored through the very Word of God. It literally became life and health to his flesh! It has been over twenty-two years since his last surgery. Praise God! We have witnessed God's promises in action. The world views sickness as a part of life and something we have no control over. God's ways are much better than that. Jesus paid a great price not just for our spiritual healing but for our physical healing. 1 Peter 2:24 (NKJV) says, "Who Himself bore our sins in His own body on the tree, that we, having died to sins, might live for righteousness—by whose stripes you were healed." John 10:10 (NKJV) says, "The thief does not come except to steal, and to kill, and to destroy. I (Jesus) have come that they may have life, and that they may have it more abundantly." We have an enemy (the devil) who is looking for any opportunity to steal from us, kill us, or destroy us. Anything less than abundance is not God's best. That's why we regard sickness as a trespasser in our home.

From the time our children were little babies and whenever sickness, fevers, or any type of childhood illnesses would try and rear their ugly heads, our first response was to pray and to speak God's healing promises over them. We declared God's Word and commanded any infections or abnormalities to cease in their bodies by the power of Jesus' name. We are definitely not against outside medical intervention and our children did take some antibiotics and other medications throughout their childhood. However, we kept in mind our help ultimately came from the Lord as we endeavored to consistently declare His restoration, healing, and wholeness over our children.

On a side note, we did have our children immunized. It is a personal choice for every parent, but whether a child is immunized or not, we will still need to exercise faith in God to take care of our children and their bodies. We always prayed prior to their doctor's appointments and declared that the immunizations would do exactly as they were designed to do without any complications or ill effects. We were also very cautious about giving them immunizations if they had a runny nose or were battling any kind of illness. Several times their shots were delayed until they were in optimal health. As a parent, we know if they are at their best or not. We've had doctors who've wanted to give our kids all kinds of shots not required by the school and most of the time we have passed on them. If we don't have a peace about something the doctor is ordering, we'll hold off on it, pray about it, and come back later if need be.

I vividly remember that as toddlers, our children would run crying to us if they scraped their knee or "bonked" their head on something. We would hold out our arms and say, "Come here! Let me pray for you." We would embrace them and say, "Father, heal their boo-boo and make them feel all better. In Jesus' name. Amen." They would soon settle down, take a breath, and walk off knowing it wasn't Mom or Dad who helped them, but it was Jesus. As they grew a little older, they would ask us to pray for them when they got hurt. Their childlike faith grasped that in times of pain, they should talk to Jesus, their Healer.

This was a very natural part of our life. We weren't trying to work anything up or put on a show. We really believe that Jesus is our Healer.

Sickness or the expectation of getting sick is not a topic of conversation in our home. If we hear the flu is going around, we'll say, "Not in our house. No plague will come near us" (Psalm 91:10). We walk in divine health in our home. That doesn't mean that we don't have opportunities where sickness tries to latch on—we are quick to resist and walk free from it (James 4:7). At the hint of a fever or a headache and before we ever head to the Ibuprofen or Tylenol bottle, we go to God and declare His healing power. We found it is a lot easier to pray at the first sign of sickness than to let it linger for days and to possibly grow into something more serious. Why not give it to God right away instead of trying to "handle it" on our own with the understanding we'll call Him if it gets too bad?

We are sure to check ourselves when sickness tries to creep in. Is God prompting us to examine the areas of diet, exercise, or rest? Are we at odds with anyone? Are we holding any bitterness in our hearts over a suffered or perceived wrong from someone? Is there someone we need to forgive? I heard a minister say once that he had seen more people healed through forgiveness than anything else. We have to be aware of any open doors that may be allowing sickness place in our homes.

Psalm 91:16 says (NIV), "With long life I will satisfy him and show him my salvation." We are promised long life and that includes our children. We don't need to sign for any sickness packages the devil sends to our door. He would have no greater pleasure than to take our children out early, and squelch the impact and destiny on this earth that God has ordered for them. I see nothing in the Bible where any of us have to die from a disease or accident. When we've lived a full age and are satisfied—like the great men of faith in the scriptures—we can lay down and peacefully transition to Heaven as we sleep, or be taken in a moment without suffering or pain.

Faith begins where the will of God is known. We cannot receive something we don't know belongs to us. Many pray to God hopeful for healing but not fully confident that they will receive it. Reading the Gospels, we see that Jesus did not come to earth to display His deity but to reveal His Heavenly Father's expressed will. Jesus did everything His Father told Him to do (John 5:19). He went about doing good and healing ALL who were oppressed of the devil for God was with Him (Acts 10:38, KJV). If it was God's will that we walk in divine healing then, it is certainly His will now for He NEVER changes (Hebrews 13:8).

Now that our children are young adults, they are praying for themselves in the area of healing. Nothing is more powerful than God's Words coming out of our children's own lips! As parents, we can surround our children with God's healing promises and a strong belief in His healing power. When sickness or disease tries to strike, our arrows can safely glide past the enemy's camp, protected by the Word of the Living God.

Some excellent resources to help grow our faith in the area of healing are as follows: *God's Creative Power for Healing* by Charles Capps and *The Believer's Authority* by Kenneth E. Hagin. Brother Keith Moore from Moore Life Ministries has free audio and video downloads available on the subject of healing. Go to moorelife.org and click on free downloads and "Healing" in the series list.

# ARROWS MUST BE AIMED

An arrow is useless unless it is pointed towards a target. It makes no sense for someone to start randomly shooting arrows without any objective or care of where they will land. An arrow was created to penetrate a premeditated destination. Just like the arrow, God has a specific path for our children to follow that will lead them to His perfect will for their lives. Jeremiah 29:11 (TLB) says, "For I know the plans I have for you, says the Lord . . . ." Since He knows the plan for our children, there is a definite direction our children will need to be aimed toward for them to meet their purpose head-on. As parents, there are things we can do to help our children perfectly align with the center of the bull's-eye.

## Raise Children with Faith and Prayer

I sat down to eat in the staff lunchroom. As I began to crunch on my salad, one by one the table began to fi ll with a group of my fellow coworkers. Most of them were ladies and as usual, our conversations were lively and mixed with laughter. A couple of the women began to discuss some of the challenges they were having with their teenage children. Nothing too serious was going on, but it was obvious from the tone of their voices they were growing weary of the constant grind of discipline. I noticed one of the younger mothers sitting silently and taking it all in. It was obvious her mind was churning and as the conversation grew to a close, she uttered, "I sure am glad I have a lot of time before my kids are teenagers." In reality, I knew she was saying, "I'm not looking forward to the teenage years!" I immediately spoke up and said, "Having teenagers is wonderful. They are the culmination of all the investment in their lives, and we are able to see the fruit of all that training. These are the years we start seeing God's purpose blossoming in them. It is an exciting time. They are more responsible than ever. They are able to drive and make decisions on their own without us having to be involved in every little aspect of their lives. There's nothing to fear." Afterwards, this young mother took me aside privately and thanked me for giving her the right perspective in raising teenagers and shining much needed truth in this area.

In the beginning of Genesis, we see God standing before the shapeless, unfruitful, dark planet of Earth. As He looked around, His first words were not "it is pitch black here! This place is a mess." He chose not to dwell on its current state. Instead, He saw the potential of Earth. Out of his very being He proclaimed, "Let there be light!" and light appeared (Genesis 1:3, JUB)! He went on to create every facet of life as we know it, using the power of His words. Because we are made in the image of God, He has given us the ability to create with our words. Hebrews 11:1 (KJV) says, "Now faith is the substance of things hoped for, the evidence of things not seen." As God's sons and daughters, it pleases Him when we tap into the realm of the unseen and by faith, watch them come to pass (Hebrews 11:6). This is especially true when it comes to raising our children. I tell new parents that having their children will be the "longest, shortest" time of their lives. We have a brief window to make the most impact on our children as possible. When they are born, they are empty vessels full of potential. As their parents, God fully expects us to call into being things that don't even exist yet in them (Romans 4:17 TPT). Raising children to be smart, responsible, mature, independent, life-giving, flourishing adult leaders isn't based on the luck of the draw or the spin of a wheel. It is being purposeful in the words we speak and the prayers that we pray over our children day after day, realizing those positive or negative words will come to pass in their lives.

The enemy will bring plenty of opportunities to worry about our children, but we don't have to live with a pervading fear that things will go wrong with them. We can cast those cares on the Lord and embrace the real truth of God's promises. We can ask God to help us see beyond any temporary negative behaviors to the big picture of His ultimate plan for them.

Kevin and I didn't raise perfect children. If they messed up, we didn't say, "We figured this would happen. We knew you were going to go off the deep end one day. Now that you're a teenager, it doesn't surprise us that you're getting more and more rebellious." This kind of talk sets our children up for failure. Our kids will mess up from time to time, but there is no need to get into fear about it. A mistake doesn't define the essence of who our children are, and it certainly doesn't define what God thinks about them. Proverbs 22:6 (NKJV) says, "Train up a child in the way he should go, and when he is old he will not depart from it." Many well-meaning people have translated this verse to say, "If I raise my children in the ways of the Lord, when they backslide they will eventually come back to the Lord." It is true that God's Word planted in our children will not return void and it is highly likely they will come back to God after their rebellion. However, this verse doesn't say the child will temporarily turn from God. We can have a full expectation that our children will continue in the ways of the Lord through childhood, and will have a strong relationship with Him in their adult years. There is no reason to believe our children ever have to run from God.

We should think about the words we speak over our children. If there is ANYTHING we would not want to come to pass, then we should NOT SAY IT! It hurts my heart to hear parents tell their children "You're a brat. You're a little devil. You're a meanie. You're up to no good. You're dumb. You're bad." I especially loathe t-shirts that say "here comes trouble." Knowing the power of our words, WHY would any parent say such foolish things?

There are some who would disagree with paying attention to EVERY word spoken from our mouths. "I'm just kidding" they may say. However, when we speak negative things over our children, even in jest, our words have the propensity to become a planted seed in their mind. As they laugh together with us, in their hearts our children may be saying "do they really think that about me?" Sarcasm usually has a hint of truth to it, and can be a way to say how we feel under the guise of a joke. Dr. Caroline Leaf, a neuroscientist and leader in how the brain functions, notes that our words have the ability to change a person's genetic expression. Negative words can damage brain cells that can make an impact on the physical body and thought processes. This toxicity creates mutated genes that can be passed on through our DNA to our children. This is why we see many children carry on the same destructive patterns of their parents. But those genetic tendencies can be broken through the Word of God.

God takes very seriously the words we speak over our children, including how we address them. When my children were small, I got into the habit of calling them "baby." I would say, "Come here, baby." "What do you need, baby?" and that continued until my oldest was almost out of middle school. One day, the Lord arrested me and said, "Stop calling them baby. They are growing into young men and ladies and they do not need any hindrances of keeping them in an immature state." It hit me that the reason I was calling them baby was because it helped me hold on to an aspect of them being little that I didn't want to let go. I've seen time after time where parents continue to call their child "pooky" or "peanut" through high school and on into adulthood. 1 Corinthians 13:11 (NKJV) says, "When I was a child, I spoke as a child, I understood as a child, I thought as a child; but when I became a man, I put away childish things." If we look at this verse from the perspective of a parent we could say, "When our child was a child, we spoke to them as a child. As they grew older, we put away that childish way of speaking to them." There's nothing worse than hearing a forty-five-year-old man being called "doodlebug" by his mother. These terms of endearment may have been okay at very early seasons in life, but as our children grow older we need to put those names aside and allow them to walk confidently into adulthood without any embarrassing attachments or stumbling blocks.

It is important to declare the best about our children and expect them to excel in life. We should want them to do better than us in all areas of life, allowing them to stand on our shoulders. We should never compete against our children, as if we had something to prove. I remember a funny movie called *Kicking and Screaming* where the father and the son seemed to always make everything a competition. This father seized opportunities to rub his son's shortcomings in his face while making himself look good. No, we aren't in a contest with our children. It's our job to help them win.

Matthew 4:4 (NKJV) says, "Man shall not live by bread alone but by every word that proceeds from the mouth of God." Our children's lives should ultimately be framed by God's words coming out of our mouths. I ran across a little booklet called *Raising Winning Kids* when Austin was very young. It was written by Cathie Dorsch, a children's minister who had a Christian television program for children called *Kids Like You*. I had no idea that this booklet would become a lifeline for me as a parent. Within the pages, now wrinkled and worn by use, were confessions based on scripture that I would declare over my children literally thousands of times. One of my favorite confessions that my children heard daily before school and knew by heart was:

> *My children's minds are anointed. They are quick to learn. They have great success in school. They never have a problem learning anything new. In all matters they're found to be ten times better than most children. Thank you, Holy Spirit, for teaching and training my children today.*

Kevin and I prayed that our children would have a different spirit about them, just like Daniel. Because of their sincere love for God and dedication to Him, we believed His favor would exalt them and place them in leadership positions. We can also speak into the atmosphere that our children are the following:

| | |
|---|---|
| *Committed to the Lord* | *Merciful* |
| *Champions* | *Successful* |
| *World Changers* | *Creative* |
| *Courteous* | *Healthy* |
| *Kind* | *Smart* |

These truths will take hold in our children and they'll naturally walk in them.

In the section "Sensitivity to the Holy Spirit," we see the importance of being in tune to what God is saying about our children in any given moment. Giving heed to those divine promptings to pray are an important responsibility as parents. We should always be ready to stand in the gap for our kids!

I have included a prayer guideline at the back of this book. Some other excellent resources to help us pray over our children are: *Raising Winning Kids* by Cathie Dorsch (may be purchased at commissionfields.com), *The Power of a Praying Parent* by Stormie Omartian (found on most online book outlets), and *Pregnancy Prayers* app for praying over our developing children in the womb (found on any digital app store).

God says He watches over His word to make sure it is fulfilled (Jeremiah 1:12, NIV). What a rewarding feeling it is to see the fruit of His word coming to pass in our children's lives. Life gets busy, but we can never neglect praying for our children and declaring God's promises for them. As we see beyond today with the eye of faith, we can have full confidence that our children's paths will be prosperous and blessed. As I told my friend at lunch that day, "there is no need to fear." When our children fail, we don't have to call it like we see it. We can call it the way God sees it. Covering our arrows with faith-filled words and Spirit-led prayers intentionally aims them towards their divine assignment.

## A Secret Weapon

I gripped the wooden pew in front of me. Every word the youth pastor uttered at our high school church camp retreat was stirring my heart. I had rededicated my life to Jesus just months before, but what he was asking us to do would be a huge leap.

It would definitely put me on the "crazy Christian" list. What would people say? What would my family say? It didn't jive with the denomination I was raised in. The youth pastor proclaimed with passion, "And if the newly formed church in Acts needed the baptism of the Holy Spirit, how MUCH MORE do we need this special infilling of the Spirit today? When God's Spirit fell on those in the upper room, they were filled with power and spoke with new tongues." And then he asked, "Who wants God's power from on High? Who needs a holy boldness and courage to be a witness for Christ? Who wants to speak in a heavenly language?" One brave soul stood up and began making their way up to the front, and then another, and then another until the entire front of the altar area was filled with spiritually hungry students ready to draw upon the Spirit of God as never before. By this time everyone who had remained in their seats had stood to their feet in support of those who were at the front. My heart said "go," but my feet and pride said "stay." As the youth pastor began to lead the students in a simple prayer asking God to fill them with His Holy Spirit, there at my seat I gently lowered my head and whispered under my breath, "I want that too, Lord. Fill me with your Spirit." Nothing spectacular happened at that moment but during that evening's service, God took the reins during worship and the special speaker never made it to the stage. I sensed God's presence as never before. Most of the students had made their way up front and I found myself down on the floor worshiping God. All of a sudden, I began speaking words that completely bypassed my mind. It was like a flood coming up from my stomach and I realized I was SPEAKING IN TONGUES! It wasn't weird. It felt like a missing piece had just clicked into place. I felt equipped and empowered with something special that I desperately needed. From that point on, I walked in a newfound confidence to bravely live out my life with Christ.

As the weeks went by, I began seeing the importance of praying in my new heavenly prayer language.

> *Likewise the Spirit also helps in our weaknesses. For we do not know what we should pray for as we ought, but the Spirit Himself makes intercession for us with groanings which cannot be uttered. Now He who searches the hearts knows what the mind of the Spirit is, because He makes intercession for the saints according to the will of God.*

—Romans 8:26-27 (NKJV)

As I began to pray out loud, the Holy Spirit was supplying the words which were in PERFECT agreement with God's will and His Word.

What a cool thing to have in our prayer arsenal as a parent! We are very limited by the scope of our minds and human thinking. We will have many opportunities with our children where we need answers and are unsure of what the best solutions are. 1 Corinthians 14:2 (NKJV) says, "For he who speaks in a tongue does not speak to men but to God, for no one understands him; however, in the spirit he speaks mysteries." Not only can we uncover mysteries relating to our children, our individual lives, and the world around us by praying in tongues, we also have a direct line of communication to the throne room of God. The devil is totally shut out to what is being said, because he can't understand this language! Therefore, he won't be able to defeat the plan of God.

My husband is constantly having to twist off bolts and screws in his auto repair shop. He can either use all of his energy cranking the bolt off by hand, or use his electric impact wrench to wind it off in seconds. That's how I look at praying with our natural mind compared to praying in the Spirit. Both work, but we can make a lot more progress when we pray in the Spirit.

What a simple prayer it was for me to ask God to baptize me with His Holy Spirit. It went something like this:

*Heavenly Father, I am Your child. I have confessed that Jesus is LORD. Now, baptize me with Your Holy Spirit. I will speak, and You will put the words on my tongue. I am baptized in the Holy Spirit, and I do speak in tongues! In Jesus' Name. Amen.*

Praying in the Spirit is a supernatural vehicle that allows us prayer access into our child's future. We can link arms with God and build a spiritual road to give them easier access to their divine destinies. We can fill in potholes, put up crucial warning signs, and avert possible collisions along the way. With this secret prayer weapon, we can strategically aim our arrows to strike their targets with magnificent intensity and purpose. For more information on this subject, I recommend the following: *Seven Vital Steps to Receiving the Holy Spirit* by Kenneth E. Hagin and *God's Will is the Holy Spirit* by Gloria Copeland. Additionally, go to KCM.org (Kenneth Copeland Ministries) and search for "Baptism of the Holy Spirit" to see previous podcasts and blogs.

## Tithing and the Blessing of God

One summer day a group of kids were hanging out at the home of James and Dawn Randolph, having fun swimming in the pool. Unbeknownst to her parents their daughter, Jaden, had gotten her hair caught in the side vent of the pool, and it sucked her head in so hard that she was unable to surface above the water. One of the children ran up to her dad and said, "Jaden is under water and not moving, and we don't think she's fooling around." He dashed to Jaden's side and pulled with all his might to free her from the immense suction coming from the pool vent. He jerked her up and out of the water and laid her on the pool deck. He began performing CPR while his wife called 911. When the first responders arrived, they immediately began working on her with their life-saving techniques. Jaden was cold, blue, unresponsive, and not breathing. She was showing all of the signs of death. After five minutes of continuous care, they had done everything they could do to bring her back. The responders knew that they would soon need to make the call that she was DOA (dead on arrival). Even if they were able to revive her, the brain damage would be so severe that she would be incapacitated for life. One of the paramedics lifted his hands off of Jaden and began to shake his head at Dawn, sending her the message that her daughter was dead.

Immediately her husband screamed out a blood curdling cry, "No Satan! You can't have my baby. We are tithers! God will rebuke you today!" The EMT said Jaden's little body jumped up about eighteen inches from the deck and came back down. She instantly stood to her feet, opened her eyes and said, "Can somebody turn off the pool please?" The paramedics transported her to the hospital for observation. When the ambulance arrived at the hospital, Jaden walked from the vehicle and into the building without assistance. The doctors asked if she was hurt in any way. She said, "No, I'm just like Jesus. I've been raised from the dead!"

One may ask, "Out of all the things this gentleman could have said in that moment, why did he shout that they were tithers?" When his child's life was on the line, he understood the power of giving God ten percent of his income and what was promised to him as a tither. In Malachi 3:11 (NKJV) God states one of the things He'll do for us when we tithe, "'And I will rebuke the devourer for your sakes, so that he will not destroy the fruit of your ground, nor shall the vine fail to bear fruit for you in the field,' says the Lord of hosts." James Randolph was able to boldly hold God at His Word, and his daughter's life was spared because he knew his tithing rights.

Malachi 3:10 (NKJV) says, "Bring all the tithes into the storehouse, that there may be food in My house, and try Me now in this, says the Lord of hosts, if I will not open for you the windows of heaven and pour out for you such blessing that there will not be room enough to receive it." Tithing is the doorway to a windfall of blessings God uses to meet our entire family's needs. Without the blessing of the Lord, all of our efforts are in vain. We are fighting an uphill battle as parents when we refuse to put God first in the area of our finances.

In Malachi 3:9 we see that when we rob God of our tithe, we open ourselves up to being cursed. God doesn't curse us, but our disobedience draws the curse upon us. Living under a curse is HARD. Everything that can go wrong will go wrong. The kids may be sick all the time. Things are going to break down all over the place. If it's not the car on the fritz, it will be the refrigerator or the air conditioning system. Money will flow out the door like it's water. But if we do things God's way, our family will have the blessing of God's protection and provision. We will have the blessing of God's promotion according to Malachi 3:12 (NKJV), "'And all nations will call you blessed, for you will be a delightful land,' says the Lord of hosts."

Our tithe is what helps our local church pay their staff, the light bill, pave the parking lot, and all of the other expenses it takes to run the church. We are equipping our church with the resources it needs to effectively propagate the Gospel of Jesus Christ to our community. I look at the tithe as a way to bless the place we are spiritually fed. God doesn't want our churches limping around and barely surviving. He is a great accountant and knows that if we all gave our ten percent, the churches would thrive, and He would be able to pour out exponential blessings on the ninety percent left of our income.

One of my favorite cakes is a carrot cake. It is three tiers of deliciousness with cream cheese frosting on top. The basic recipe of any cake consists of flour, butter, sugar, and eggs. What if we decided to leave the flour out? It wouldn't look like much of a cake and it surely would not taste like one. It seems silly to omit such a key ingredient, doesn't it? As parents, we must not view tithing as an option for our lives. Just like the cake, we can't exclude this important foundational ingredient and then wonder why our cake flopped. I have prayed and spoken with a lot of people who were in financial duress. They were hoping I could say a magic-wand prayer and all of their money problems would disappear. God cannot violate his covenant promise of increase when we refuse to use the key that unlocks the door of blessing. We can't circumvent tithing and fully expect all of the benefits that come along with it.

For some, giving ten percent of their income seems exorbitant and way beyond their means. They rationalize, thinking God will give them a tithing pass because of their financial predicament. I think about the widow woman in Mark 12:41-44 who gave her last two copper coins (worth less than a penny) in the offering. Jesus sat there and watched her sacrificially give these precious mites. Instead of Jesus telling this woman He would not expect her to give because of her poverty-stricken condition, He allowed her to invest all that she had. He knew the power of giving and that this extraordinary act of faith would set a blessing in motion that this dear lady would not have room enough to contain! When God asks us to tithe, He is not trying to take something from us. He's trying to give something to us!

We can equip our children with all of the natural resources and skills for them to succeed, but if we disregard putting God first in the tithe, we are doing them a great disservice. Our giving intertwines with everything we do and impacts every aspect of our child's life. This simple act of honoring God strategically aims our arrows with the provision, protection, and promotion they need to masterfully arrive at their God-given destiny.

For an abundance of resources regarding tithing, go to KCM.org (Kenneth Copeland Ministries) and search for "Tithing" to see previous podcasts and blogs. Also, Google search for "Jesse Duplantis Tithing" or "Keith Moore Tithing" for videos and blogs.

# ARROWS MUST BE TIMED PROPERLY

Once an arrow has been positioned towards a target, the next few moments are crucial in determining exactly when to let go of the bow string to allow the arrow to discharge. Many different factors play into getting the arrow to the center of the mark. The weather and wind must be accurately assessed, and compensations must be made to prevent the arrow from drifting and missing the target. Extreme patience must be exerted while waiting for some targets to come into plain view in order to get the best shot. If we allow our anticipation to get to us, we could prematurely release the arrow and fall dismally short of our objective. If we second-guess the shot—allowing apprehension to paralyze us—the target and window of opportunity could pass us by.

> *There is a right time for everything, and everything on earth will happen at the right time.*
>
> —Ecclesiastes 3:1 (ERV)

As parents, it's important to recognize the different seasons of maturity in our arrows and confidently release them into greater levels of responsibility at just the right time.

## We Can't Force Seasons

One of my favorite childhood memories are the Christmases spent at my grandmother and granddad's house. The food was out of this world, and there was a flurry of activity with all of the family gathered. As always a cardboard table was set up with a brand new puzzle ready to be conquered. When we'd dump the pieces out on the table, the job seemed like a huge undertaking. It was a bit overwhelming seeing the hundreds of pieces scattered without any rhyme or reason to them. We'd carefully look at the picture on the box and plan out a strategy of how to put the puzzle together. One person would direct and say, "You take the part with the leaves and I'll work on the edges." Our eyes would dart over the pile and by a meticulous process of elimination, we'd begin finding pieces for our areas of the puzzle. Hours would go by and with relentless determination, we'd keep going. Like tireless soldiers, we would barely take time for bathroom breaks or a drink of water. It was pure joy to finally find a piece I was hunting, as I quickly grabbed it and placed it into position. Most times, the piece would slide right into place. But every now and then I'd realize that although it was super close, the piece didn't fit. Disgusted, I'd push it in harder thinking "maybe the machining was off, and I just need to force it in a bit." It took so long to find that piece and I really wanted it to be the one. Although the edges weren't aligning perfectly and it bubbled up a little, at a glance it fit and that was good enough for me. As time went by, I came across the correct piece to go in that slot. I switched it out with the obvious ill-fitting one, and it slid right into place. It brought instant relief and satisfaction knowing that area was now as it should be. Matthew 11:28 (MSG) says, "Walk with me and work with me—watch how I do it. Learn the unforced rhythms of grace." God has ordained a special grace for our children that when followed will guide them to the right people, at the right place, and the right time. Like the wrong piece of a puzzle, our children's lives won't have to be shoved into position. God will make things happen for them.

Most parents believe the best in their child and it's hard watching them get bypassed for something that is really important to them whether it be a musical solo or a lead in a play. Although it can be tough, we have to be willing to let God initiate their promotion. 1 Peter 5:6 (ASV) says, "Therefore humble yourselves under the mighty hand of God, that He may exalt you at the proper time." Elbowing our way in to ensure our children have a fair shake is crossing the line. If we develop a habit of pressuring leadership to succumb to our wishes, it will usually generate an entitlement mentality in our children of "they owe me." As parents, we have to steer our children to trust in God and not in the actions of men. My pastor, Brett Jones, says, "Everyone is vying for first chair but without second and third chair there are no harmonies. They make the sound all the more beautiful." We can help our children embrace the importance of their roles and teach them how they can give their best to the team. It's all about perspective!

The amount of play time our kids receive in sports can be a bone of contention. We may give way to anger thinking it's all due to team politics. In reality, it may be that our child is not that good. I think about American Idol and some of these poor kids who have grown up in small towns who were the star of their ten-member choir—their parents, family members, and friends *knew* they were destined for fame. During the audition, the judges look for a certain caliber of vocalist and when the contestant doesn't make it to the next level, he or she are often bewildered and crushed. As parents, it's actually to our children's advantage to have a different set of eyes on them other than us. Because we are vested in our kids, we may be blinded to some things due to our love and care for them. We have to be open to allow our kids to shift direction into new territories and pursue things they may be much better suited for.

Not only do we have to resist the temptation to force others to place our kids in certain positions, we have to be cautious to not force our children into roles they're not prepared to handle. Several leadership opportunities and experiences arose that I felt my children would want to pursue. The temptation to push my children into doing those things was there. However, I had to take a step back and allow them to make the choice. I understood that if they felt pressured to take on these roles, they wouldn't give it their all. Plus, them saying "yes" to an undesired position could hinder them from embracing an opportunity that would have yielded far more personal growth. When our children are ready, God will slide them right into the perfect place!

One evening as I rocked my then three-month-old daughter—DeLaney—to sleep, I felt an overwhelming sense to prophesy over her. By God's divine inspiration, I began to boldly declare, "DeLaney, you shall have the heart of a psalmist. You will write songs that come directly from the throne room of Heaven and you will lead the nations in worship." I had never experienced anything like this with my other two children, but I knew this proclamation was straight from the Lord. As the years went by, like Mary the mother of Jesus, I hid this message about my daughter in my heart (Luke 2:19). God had clued me in about her destiny and by faith I knew it would happen. I could have shared God's plans with DeLaney as soon as she was old enough to understand, but I chose to wait fifteen years. By then, she was passionately pursuing music and was leading worship regularly in youth group and at youth camp. She expressed her ultimate desire in being a worship leader. When I revealed what God spoke to her as an infant, it was confirmation of the direction she was already headed. I never wanted to prematurely disclose this information and it end up being a manipulative tool to obligate her to a musical calling. I was cautious to not force this season to come to pass in DeLaney's life. Instead, I patiently waited for God to lay the crucial foundation that would sustain His plans for her.

In Genesis 37, we read about young Joseph and the vivid dream he had where his brothers, mother, and father bowed down to him in honor. His brothers were already jealous because they thought their father loved him more, so this dream really ticked them off. They ended up secretly selling Joseph into slavery and making up an elaborate story to their father about how Joseph was murdered by a ferocious animal. Joseph was sold to a high-ranking man in Egypt and his wife falsely accused Joseph of rape. He was sent to jail and the prison warden placed him in charge, over all of the other prisoners. Through an interaction between two of Pharaoh's servants who were imprisoned, Joseph became the second in command of Egypt. Joseph's dream inevitably came to pass but it took fourteen years! Psalm 105:19 (NLT) says, "Until the time came to fulfill his dreams, the Lord tested Joseph's character." God gave him numerous opportunities to stretch and grow in character until he was ready to carry the weight of this influential position. John Wooden quotes, "Ability may get you to the top, but it takes character to keep you there." Sustaining a dream is much more important than achieving it!

It is to our children's advantage to allow God to do a perfect work in them throughout each and every season of life.

*For you know that when your faith is tested it stirs up power within you to endure all things. And then as your endurance grows even stronger it will release perfection into every part of your being until there is nothing missing and nothing lacking.*

—James 1:3-4 (TPT)

Helping our children fast forward through times of testing will not only minimize their spiritual stamina but hinder them from possessing God's best for them. We must be willing to wait alongside them, watching for His green light to enter the next season.

Ecclesiastes 3 heralds, "Everything has a season." We cannot coerce a fruit to ripen on the vine. We cannot will it to grow any faster. We cannot force what is not ready to be birthed. If we allow God to properly develop character, endurance, and passion in our arrows they will arrive right where they need to be at the appointed time.

## Boyfriends/Girlfriends and Marriage

As I walked down the hall after our Wednesday night church service, I heard a young mother's voice behind me say, "Go hold your husband's hand." Immediately, I heard the sound of tiny feet running like the wind. A little toddler girl darted around me to meet up with the sweet toddler boy walking with his parents several yards in front of me. The two of them clasped hands and skipped playfully down the hall. Both sets of parents began to laugh as one said, "We've got them trained, don't we?" One of the mothers said, "Well, they just need to realize they were made for each other. They don't know it yet, but they're going to get married someday!" My eyes met with one of the couples and I flashed them a hollow smile as I pushed the exit door to head to the parking lot. "Wow,"

I thought. "They're match-making their babies." These parents probably thought their attempts were harmless and all in good fun, but they didn't realize they had carelessly ventured into sacred territory.

Next to making Jesus the Lord of our lives, choosing a spouse is one of the most important decisions we will ever make. It is serious business! Our job as parents isn't to set our children up with a mate but to prepare our children to be a mate. The best gift they could ever give to their future spouse is knowing who they are and what they are called to do. Unfortunately, I've seen my fair share of newly married couples who are clueless about where they are going in life and hoping their mate will show them the way. With fifty percent of marriages ending in divorce, it's worth the effort to help our children develop into purpose-filled, confident, and independent adults. These characteristics will lay a strong foundation for their future marriages.

A prime window for our children's growth is the time before they graduate high school. This is a crucial period for them to expand their social skills, learn greater responsibility, grow in education, and mature in their thinking and spirituality. Kevin and I made it very clear to our children that their main focus as they were going through school was to develop themselves and not look for a potential mate. Although it was against the social norm, we asked them to not have a boyfriend or girlfriend before graduating from high school. We frequently discussed the benefits of concentrating on themselves and gaining clarity for their futures. They understood that their prospective mate would be abundantly blessed by the efforts they were making towards the marriage they would one day share. We helped our children dream about who they would be to their spouse, and not just who their spouse would be. The satisfaction of gaining valuable skills to become the best husband or wife superceded any minor feelings of loss they had of not having a boyfriend or girlfriend.

Many teens are involved in boyfriend/girlfriend relationships, but most are not mature enough to handle a "love interest." I romanticized all through elementary and middle school about finding a boyfriend in high school and wearing his class ring. About halfway through my freshman year, I began to panic because my boyfriend had not surfaced yet. I had a certain type in mind, but soon tossed all preconceived desires aside and was ready to settle for just about any guy who was breathing. Almost immediately upon revising my standards, I had my boyfriend! I clung to this guy for the rest of my high school years, although I knew in my heart he was not good for me. This relationship opened me up to temptations I shouldn't have been dealing with at that time. I ended up with a serious soul tie, untold stress, loss of focus, and extreme drama all just to wear the coveted class ring!

When our children share stories with us about classmates' love relationships that are going awry, we can use these as teaching moments. We can reemphasize that their school years should be full of fun, friends, and focus. We can show them that hearts are like fine china—when they are carelessly given away, they can easily be shattered. Hearts that are protected and respectfully handled will remain beautiful vessels of honor to be treasured for generations to come.

It is highly likely that our children will be attracted to someone of the opposite sex prior to graduating from high school. When this happens, we shouldn't freak out about it. We never want to send the message that those feelings of attraction are somehow wrong. Kevin and I playfully teased our kids when we noticed their interest in someone. I've seen children who have grown up in very strict religious settings where their parents wouldn't even discuss the opposite sex. When their children looked at a boy or girl, they were doomed to experience God's wrath. It was ingrained in their minds that this type of desire was hellish and wrong. We definitely don't want to subconsciously train our kids to not like the opposite sex! It's not our aim to squelch those desires but to help our children put them in their proper place for this time in their lives.

Prayer is key during this season because of the extreme social pressure for our children to be in a romantic relationship as early as elementary school! Kevin and I always prayed for our children to be wise beyond their years and for them to clearly see the foolishness of the world around them. We also began praying for their mates when our children were babies. We prayed for their health, for their spiritual growth, and for their parents who were tasked with the monumental responsibility to raise them in the admonition of the Lord. I specifically remember several years ago when I had an extreme burden to pray for Austin's future wife. I told him that evening that I had prayed for his wife and that she would be spiritually strong, a wonderful helpmeet to him, and would be a full of wisdom. Austin said, "Thank you for doing that, Mom. Did you happen to pray that she would be pretty, too?" I just had to laugh, but he was right. We grabbed hands and immediately thanked God for his beautiful wife!

Kevin and I focused on the type of qualities our children should be looking for in their mates. We encouraged our daughters to not only look for a man who loved God but also for someone with a strong work ethic. Dreamers are very important, but the doers are the ones who get the job done (James 1:22, KJV). They should not have a propensity for laziness and be someone they will have to constantly poke and prod to accomplish something. It will be easy to see the trajectory of their potential husband's life based on the choices they have already made. Even if their current career path is not what their ultimate dream is, are they giving their best without grumbling and complaining? Are they doing it with excellence? Are they being proactive and not waiting on life to just happen? If they are at our house for dinner, will they clear their dishes off the table? Will they notice that the kitchen trash can is full and take out the trash without being asked to do so? Everything speaks!

We inspired Austin to choose a woman who knows who she is in Christ Jesus, and is confident in her calling. She should not look to our son to complete her and drain him for her worth and purpose. He would never be able to give a woman like that enough love to fill that type of longing in her soul. She should be an encourager and a strong support for him.

God's gift of marriage is a beautiful thing and unfortunately, something that mainstream society does not honor or hold in high esteem. In our Member Care department, we are privileged to assist thirty plus couples per year with their premarital counseling. Out of those couples, close to eighty percent are living together and ninety percent are not abstaining from sexual relations. We also know of couples who are living together and not interested in being married due to their ability to get food stamps and free healthcare for their children as a single parent. They've given into a lie that their needs won't be met if they do things the right way.

Children are being bombarded with the idea that sex before marriage is not only acceptable, but it's a standard for relationships. 1 Corinthians 6:18 (KJV) says, "Flee fornication . . . ." Fornication is not a word we hear a lot in this day and age, but it means having sexual relations outside of the covenant of marriage. We can show our children that God provides a covering and protection for us when we do things His way. We can also help them to put some guidelines in place when they do begin dating, to ward off unnecessary temptations. They can focus on going out in groups and not spending a lot of alone time with the person they are dating. Also, if they have too much time on their hands and don't have a lot of extracurricular activities to occupy their day, they need to get a part-time job. It is not good for our kids to have copious amounts of time to burn as it may lead to them getting "burned."

God intended sex to be a binder between a husband and wife that makes them one flesh (Mark 10:8-9, NIV). It creates an intimacy that is a powerful weapon against the devil and his tactics. When a married couple comes together in prayer, they will move mountains as they walk in supernatural agreement. We can teach our children that staying within God's guidelines in their relationships will prevent all kinds of problems down the road and yield abundant blessings in their lives.

If children remain focused on developing themselves through school and not in finding a boyfriend or girlfriend, they will be wide open to vital direction from the Lord. They'll be able to freely pursue their dreams without having to juggle a relationship that usually won't last. They won't have to endure unwanted emotional baggage when a breakup occurs. Though our arrows may be flying against extreme cultural opposition, waiting for the appropriate time to pursue a mate will give them the momentum needed to strike their destined target with maximum force.

## Seedtime and Harvest

We were right smack in the middle of rush hour traffic. The kids and I had made a mad dash to the grocery store to pick up a few items for dinner and now we were stuck. Every vehicle was wedged in tight with nowhere to go. We anxiously waited to inch forward with every cycle of the traffic light. A few unfortunate folks were patiently waiting to edge out into the traffic flow from a side parking lot from another business. I watched their failed attempts to make eye contact with the drivers to allow them access on the road. Looking straight ahead, the drivers would not even acknowledge that these people existed as they hurriedly drove down the street. Something began stirring in my heart and I realized that I had a perfect teaching opportunity for my children. As I neared the area I said, "Kids, watch this. No one is letting these people out but we're going to do it. This will be a seed. Whenever we need to get out on the road, God will make a way for us." From that day forward, every time we needed to turn into a line of traffic, within a few seconds, someone would always come and let us in. I would make a point to say, "Look kids! Look what God has done for us! We are reaping a harvest on letting people out on the road!"

> *God's kingdom realm is like someone spreading seed on the ground. He goes to bed and gets up, day after day, and the seed sprouts and grows tall, though he knows not how. All by itself it sprouts, and the soil produces a crop; first the green stem, then the head on the stalk, and then the fully developed grain in the head. Then, when the grain is ripe, he immediately puts the sickle to the grain, because harvest time has come.*
>
> —Mark 4:26-29 (TPT)

God's Kingdom operates on the law of seedtime and harvest. Every day, we hold seeds of potential in our hands that when planted can yield all types of consequences in our lives. In Christian circles when we hear about planting seed, many times it is associated with money. Although giving our finances can yield a return, it is not the only form of seed. We can teach our children that things as simple as showing kindness, respect, and humility are powerful seeds that can produce reciprocating behaviors from other people. Negative actions are also seeds that can bring about unfavorable conditions in our children's lives. For every action, whether good or bad, a rippling impact is made not only on others but on ourselves, also. That is why Jesus exhorted us to "do for other people what you would like to have them do for you" (Luke 6:31, NLV).When we use this admonishment as a filter for our actions, we will always be planting good seed!

Our children witnessed the return on all kinds of seed Kevin and I planted through the years. Kevin is a mechanic and we've purchased vehicles to repair and sell for a profit. We've given some of these vehicles to people and in return, neither we nor our children have ever been without a good quality car. Many of the vehicles we have driven over the years were given to us! We made sure our children understood the law of return that was happening to us.

Oral Roberts University has an excellent scholarship program for students called "The Whole Person Scholarship." Knowing that our children would one day attend college, Kevin and I purposefully began giving towards this scholarship when our children were young. Each time we gave, we gave it as seed for our children's college to be paid in full. Two of our children are now in college and our youngest will be attending college in the fall. Each one of them have received scholarships, grants, and internships that will completely pay for their tuition, and room and board. DeLaney, will be attending Oral Roberts University and she was a recipient of the Whole Person Scholarship! Is this a coincidence? Certainly not! We fully expected this to happen! Our children knew that mom and dad had been planting seed all along and that God would take care of every financial need they had for school.

We have a responsibility as parents to communicate the Word of God to our children and teach them how to apply it in their everyday lives. Seedtime and harvest are an integral part of our walk with God. Galatians 6:7-8 (TPT) says, "Make no mistake about it, God will never be mocked! For what you plant will always be the very thing you harvest. The harvest you reap reveals the seed that was planted." Our children need to be consciously aware that in time they will always reap whatever they sow. When our arrows make harvest-based choices, they will open themselves up to supernatural progress while speeding toward their destiny.

# ARROWS MUST BE RELEASED

I left late from the office one evening and the sun had been down for a while. It was a clear night and the moon was shining brightly in the sky. I pulled into the driveway of my home and turned off the ignition as I usually did. Before I opened the car door I felt a holy hush come over me. In the silence, the Lord directed my attention to the two-bedroom windows lit above our garage. The scene was nothing out of the ordinary. I had pulled into our driveway hundreds of times and saw the same familiar glow coming from these windows. Today there was something different about them. The sobering realization hit me that these windows were illuminated because my son and daughter were in their rooms, most likely doing their homework. I sat there for a long time, fi xing my gaze, and trying to etch this solemn memory in my mind. I prayed, "God, help me to remember this, because I know one day these windows will be dark." I worshiped Him for blessing Kevin and me with our children, and for the "window" of time he had given us with them.

As I write this, one of those windows has already grown dim. Austin has been attending Texas Tech University in Lubbock, TX for the past two years. Before he left I was asked, "Aren't you going to miss him?" Of course, I was going to miss him!  We all had a green light though, and were filled with peace about his college choice. We knew he would be great, and do great things as God continued to direct his path.

Psalm 127:4-5 (NIV) says, "Like arrows in the hands of a warrior are children born in one's youth. Blessed is the man whose quiver is full of them." A quiver is a container that carries the arrows. It is usually cylindrical in shape and has an attached strap that can be slung over the back. Its placement is such where one can reach back and grab an arrow with ease. The arrows were never meant to stay in the quiver. The quiver was a temporary holding place to protect the arrows until it was time to release them. As parents, it's a temptation to want to hold tight to our arrows and keep them safely by our side. "What if they leave forever? Where will they go? I will miss them too much. It will be too painful to let them go. What will I do with my life now?" are all thoughts that may hinder our arrows from their mighty day of release. In reality, this is the day we have been shooting for. This is the mission they've been destined for. This is the culmination of all the hugs, the kisses, and the small corrections we've made day in and day out. We've been protecting them, but we've also been preparing them. Our arrows were made to fly, to stealthily soar throughout the earth. Our focus must go beyond the arrow we have in our hands to the target it will one day meet.

I know families who are so close that they would never think of leaving each other to live in another city. I would love for my children to live in the area and see my future grandchildren often, but if God calls them to another place, Kevin and I are okay with that. As parents, we can't allow our emotions to get in the way of our children's destinies. We need to be their greatest cheerleaders and never, intentionally nor unintentionally, make them feel guilty for following the plans and purposes of the Lord. How terrible would it be to find out in eternity that we prompted our children to bypass their highest and best calling because we were selfish? We never want to hold our children back from all that God has created them to be.

Our arrows are on loan to us from God. He has helped us craft them, balance them, sharpen them, aim them, and wait for just the right time to release them.

> *I admit that I haven't yet acquired the absolute fullness that I'm pursuing, but I run with passion into his abundance so that I may reach the purpose that Jesus Christ has called me to fulfill and wants me to discover. I don't depend on my own strength to accomplish this; however I do have one compelling focus: I forget all of the past as I fasten my heart to the future instead. I run straight for the divine invitation of reaching the heavenly goal and gaining the victory-prize through the anointing of Jesus.*
> —Philippians 3:12-14 (TPT)

The Kingdom of God is all about advancement. It's not about looking behind but pressing forward. We can't hold our children back by grieving the childhood years that are no more. Our arrows are not boomerangs to casually drift and come right back to us. Our children must be allowed the liberty to advance with their hearts fastened to their futures. No matter how difficult, we must take a deep breath and without hesitation release the bow and let our arrows fly.

# ARROWS MUST BE TRUSTED

What a satisfying experience to witness our arrows propelling towards their God-given purpose. It may take a moment to comprehend that they are flying without us. With all faith and certainty, they must be trusted to do what they were made to do. They were born for this.

Last year I wrote the following in my journal about my children: "Life started moving so quickly. I realized that there were things happening in my children's lives that only God himself could order and direct. His teaching, and training, and directing started to overtake mine and the great handoff began. I didn't see it coming. I didn't even know to expect it. But there it was. They were living, and moving, and having their being in Him. He was having talks with them that I could never say or even think to say. Almost every decision they were making met our approval. Our no's and maybe's became resounding yeses as the decisions they were making were full of wisdom and God's direction."

When our arrows begin that blessed flight, we are not abandoning them and we can be assured they are not gliding alone. God's faithful presence will always abide with our children, even after we're gone. I love Psalms 103:15-17 (TPT),

*Our days are so few, and our momentary beauty so swiftly fades away! Then all of a sudden, we're gone, like grass clippings blown away in a gust of wind, taken away to our appointment with death, leaving nothing to show that we were here. But Lord, your endless love stretches from one eternity to the other, unbroken and unrelenting toward those who fear you and those who bow face down in awe before you.* ***Your faithfulness to keep every gracious promise you've made passes from parents, to children, to grandchildren, and beyond.***

Hebrews 12:2 (NKJV) says, "Looking unto Jesus, the author and finisher of our faith . . . ." When we release our arrows, we have to trust the process of letting go and allowing them to do what they were created to do. But most all, we must trust that what God has started in our children He WILL bring to completion.

# A NEW START

After reading this book you may say, "I haven't been the kind of parent I know I should be." This book was not written to bring condemnation but to bring hope and inspiration. If you've messed up in the area of parenting, the great news is that you have the opportunity to start fresh today. Like my parents, maybe you just didn't have the resources available to make the right decisions with your children.

One of the first decisions to set yourself on the right path is to make Jesus the Lord of your life. Without His help, we are all destined for a life of confusion and instability. Romans 10:9 (NKJV) says, "If you confess with your mouth the Lord Jesus and believe in your heart that God has raised Him from the dead, you will be saved."

It all starts with a simple prayer:

> *Heavenly Father, I come to You in the Name of Jesus. Your Word says, according to Romans 10:9, "If I confess with my mouth the Lord Jesus, and believe in my heart that God has raised him from the dead, I shall be saved." I do that now. I confess that Jesus is Lord, and I believe in my heart that God raised Him from the dead. I am now reborn! I am a Christian—a child of Almighty God! I am saved! I surrender my life to you. Take my life and do something with it. In Jesus' name. Amen.*

If we've disobeyed God in certain areas of parenting, 1 John 1:9 (NKJV) says, "If we confess our sins, He is faithful and just to forgive us our sins and to cleanse us from all unrighteousness." We can simply say, "God, I ask you to forgive me for ______________, and I ask that you cleanse me from all unrighteousness. Help me to do better, Lord. In Jesus' name. Amen."

God is endlessly committed to our success as parents and as individuals. As we surrender everything to Him, He will show us all we need to know.

# BIBLE PRAYERS AND CONFESSIONS

*Dear God, I ask that you give my children spiritual wisdom and insight, so they might grow in their knowledge of You. I pray that their hearts will be flooded with light so that they can understand the confident hope You have called them to. May they grasp the inheritance you have given them in the saints and realize the exceeding greatness of Your power in their lives. In Jesus name. Amen.*

—EPHESIANS 1:16-22

*Dear God, I pray that out of Your glorious riches You may strengthen my children with power through Your Spirit in their inner being, so that Christ may dwell in their hearts through faith. And I pray that they would be rooted and established in love and have the power, together with all the Lord's holy people, to grasp how wide and long and high and deep is the love of Christ, and to know this love that surpasses knowledge—that they may be filled to the measure of all the fullness of God. Lord, I ask that you do immeasurably more than my children could ever ask or imagine, according to Your power that is at work within them. In Jesus name. Amen.*

—EPHESIANS 3:16-20

*My children's minds are anointed. They are quick to learn. They have great success in school. They never have a problem learning anything new. In all matters they're found to be ten times better than most children. Thank you, Holy Spirit, for teaching and training my children today.*

—1 COR 2:16, DANIEL 1:18-21, EPHESIANS 4:23

*My children love the Lord and delight in Him. They cherish His words and are blessed beyond expectation. They are prosperous, influential, and experience God's favor. My children are wise, and great blessing and wealth fills their houses. They are never stingy, but they are a source of blessing and are extremely generous. They always conduct their affairs with honesty and truth. Their circumstances will never shake them, and they will be a lasting example to everyone around them. My children shall not live in fear or dread of the future, but their hearts will remain firm and steady, ever secure in faith.*

—PSALM 112 (TPT). PSALM 37:26 (TPT)

*My children walk carefully, living a life with honor, purpose, and courage. They do not tolerate evil. They are filled with wisdom and discernment, and make the very most of their time on earth, seizing every God-given opportunity. They are not foolish or thoughtless, but they understand and firmly grasp what the will of the Lord is for their lives.*

—EPHESIANS 5:15-17 (AMPC)

*My children embrace God's miracles and demonstrations of His power. Their rising generation witnesses the glorious wonders He's famous for. The gifts of the Spirit are in full operation in my children's lives. God's sweet beauty rests upon them and gives them favor. God works within my children and brings them success in all that they do.*

—PSALM 90:16-17 (TPT)

*My children live honorably, surrounded by the light of this new day. They do not live in the darkness of drunkenness, debauchery, promiscuity, sensuality, argumentativeness, or jealousy. Instead they are fully immersed in the Lord Jesus Christ, and don't waste a moment's thoughts on the former life of sin they may have once experienced.*

—ROMANS 13:13-14 (TPT)

*My children don't give in to foolish relationships that corrupt good morals and character. They always come back to their senses and awaken to what is right. My children are always at the right place, at the right time, with the right people, doing the right thing!*

—1 CORINTHIANS 15:33-34 (TPT)

*My children listen to God's correction and supernatural discernment enters their heart. They are growing wise with understanding and remain faithful to God's instruction. My children reign in life because they do everything God teaches them, always remembering His words. Seeking God's wisdom is their main priority and it protects them, exalts them, leads them to honor, and brings great favor in their lives.*

—PROVERBS 4 (TPT)

*My children walk free from grief, sickness, weakness, sorrows, and pains because Jesus bore every one of these things on the Cross. Because of the wounds of Jesus, my children are released from every sin and every sting of guilt. Because of the punishment Jesus received, my children walk in peace and total well-being. Because of the stripes Jesus took upon His back, my children are healed and made whole in their spirit, soul, and body.*

—ISAIAH 53:4-5 (AMPC)

*Lord I praise you and I will not forget to declare every one of your benefits over my children. You forgive every sin and heal them from every disease. You redeem their life from destruction and crown them with your loving kindness and compassion. You satisfy their desires with good things and their youth is renewed like the eagles.*

—PSALM 103:2-5 (NIV)

*My children live in the safe place of the Most High God and are hidden in His shadow. They are kept safe under the covering of God's massive arms, far from the traps of the enemy or any false accusations against them, or sickness that would try to kill them. They will never have to worry about an attack of demonic forces coming against them nor fear the spirit of darkness. In times of disaster with thousands and thousands being killed, my children will remain unscathed and unharmed. My children are protected by God's holy angels; they are with my children wherever they go. If my children walk into a trap, they'll be there to keep them from stumbling. My children will walk away unharmed among the fiercest powers of darkness. Because my children delight in God as their great love, He will protect them. He will set them in a high place, safe and secure before His face. He will answer them when they pray and cry for help. They will always find and feel the presence of God, even in the times of pressure and trouble. God will be their glorious hero and satisfy them with a long, full life.*

—PSALM 91 (TPT)

*Because the life of God abides in my children, so does his light. His light within them shines so brightly that the darkness will never overpower them. Nothing shall be able to snuff out God's light within them*

—JOHN 1: 5 (AMPC)

*My children are anointed by God and because the Holy Spirit resides on the inside of them, they are not left in the dark about anything. They know things in their hearts that their natural mind doesn't even comprehend yet. They walk in complete freedom, and fully recognize the difference between truth and lies*

—1 JOHN 2:20-21, 27 (NKJV)

*My children walk in spiritual maturity and are not deceived by clever people who try to make them believe things that are not true. They are not easily confused by cunning liars focused to mislead them with ideas contradictory to the Word of God. My children remain strong and always speak the message of truth, because they genuinely love people. They are growing up vigorously healthy in God*

—EPHESIANS 4:14-15 (NIV)

# ACKNOWLEDGMENTS

**With special thanks to:**

My children—Austin, Kamryn, and DeLaney—and future grandchildren, great-grandchildren, great-great grandchildren and beyond (my arrows). This book was written as a legacy for you. I pray it equips you with the spiritual and natural insight you need when raising your own children. The best way to honor us as parents and grandparents is to love and serve the Lord with all your hearts, and to raise your children to know Him. God will be faithful to help you with your own arrows, just like He has been with us.

My husband, Kevin, for being my helper, my confidante, and strength. You'll always be beautiful in my eyes.

My mother, Darla Stookey. Your obedience to follow Christ changed the entire trajectory of my life.

My fathers, Lloyd Watts and Jack Stookey, who are both now in Heaven. Thank you for loving me. I know you always did.

My mother-in-law and father-in law, Bruce and Doris Schafer. Thank you for your love for God's Word and being Spirit led in your prayers for our family.

My spiritual mother and father, Pastors John B. and Debbie Lowe II. Only eternity knows the impact you have made on my life and those around you.

My best friend, Denise Dietz. Thank you for being a cheerleader, a vision processor, and a constant sounding board. I'll always be waiting for you on the front porch.

My brother, Brenden Stookey and my sisters—Sheila Boyer, Kristyn Lester, and Summer Earls. Thank you for putting up with me all these years. I consider you a gift from God and I treasure you.

My pastors, Simeon and Sonya Young. Your creative effort, design work, and editing skill brought my book to life. Because of you, I am holding my dream.

My pastors, Brett and Gizelle Jones. Your belief in me and the investments you have made in my life pushed me to be greater and do greater.

My pastors, Scott and Melanie Jones. Your loving and genuine support of me and my family have been stabilizing pillars that have helped us achieve more than we ever could have dreamed.

My pastors, Keith and Dana Cistrunk. You have taught me well. Thank you for not just telling me how but showing me how to love and care for people according to God's Word.

Cathie Dorsch, for writing a life-changing mini booklet called, Raising Winning Kids, that I still use as a resource to this day. Whatever harvest is coming from my children, you'll have a share in their reward.

My spiritual mentors, Brother Kenneth and Sister Gloria Copeland, Pastors George and Terri Pearsons, Brother Jesse and Cathy Duplantis, Brother Keith and Phyllis Moore, and Brother Kenneth E. Hagin, Sr. and the Hagin family. Thank you for boldly declaring God's truth on this earth. From generation to generation, my family will still be gleaning from the uncompromised Word of God you have faithfully seeded into our hearts.

# NOTES

**Discipline**

Swann, David and Roxanne. Guarantee Your Child's Success. Tulsa: Harrison House, Inc., 1990. Print. p. 59.

**Identity**

The Lion King. Dir. Roger Allers and Rob Minkoff. Walt Disney Pictures, 1994. Film.

**Family Devotions**

Copeland, Kenneth and Gloria. Load Up Devotional. Tulsa: Harrison House, Inc., 2012. Print.

**Let Children See Us Read our Bible, Pray and Praise God**

Nolte, Dorothy Law. "Children Learn What They Live – Complete Version", www.empowermentresources.com/info2/childrenlearn-long_version.html. Gill, A. L.

God's Promises for Your Every Need. Published for the Billy Graham Evangelistic Association by Thomas Nelson, 2008. Print.

**Spending Time with Our Children**

Dobson, Dr. James. Bringing Up Boys. Wheaton: Tyndale House Publishers, Inc., 2001. Print. pp. 88-89.

**Christmas Traditions**

Edwards, Corey. The Christmas Lizard. Tulsa: Honor Books, 2000. Print.

**Love Our Spouse**

Desai , Amy. "Who Gets Divorced?" Focus on the Family, 29 Nov. 2018, www.focusonthefamily.com/marriage/divorce-and-infidelity/ should-i-get-a-divorce/who-gets-divorced. "Financial Peace University." Dave Ramsey Homepage, www.daveramsey.com/fpu/.

**Suicide**

"Youth Suicide Statistics." Parent Resource Program, prp.jasonfoundation.com/facts/youth-suicide-statistics/.

**Friends**

Laura, et al. "94% Of Adult Christians Made Their Decision under the Age of 18."
A Mother Far from Home, 20 Apr. 2013, amotherfarfromhome.com/94-of-christians-were-saved-before-18-years-of-age/.

**Budgets**

"Money Ruining Marriages in America: A Ramsey Solutions Study." Ramsey Solutions. Ramsey Solutions, 8 Feb. 2018, www.daveramsey.com/pr/money-ruining-marriages-in-america."Financial Peace University." Dave Ramsey Homepage, www.daveramsey. com/fpu/.

**Choosing Your Emotions**

Covey, Stephen R. The 7 Habits of Highly Effective People: Powerful Lessons in Personal Change. New York: Simon & Schuster. 1989, 2004. Print. pp. 65-94. Koch, Ruth N., and Kenneth C. Haugk. Speaking the Truth in Love: How to Be an Assertive Christian. St. Louis: Stephen Ministries, 1992. Print. p. 32.

### Healer in the House

Capps, Charles. God's Creative Power for Healing. Tulsa: Harrison House Publishing. Print. 1991.

Hagin, Kenneth E. The Believer's Authority. Tulsa: Kenneth Hagin Ministries; 2nd edition. Print. 1985.

### Raise Children in Faith and Prayer

Kenneth Copeland Ministries and Dr. Caroline Leaf. "You Can Change Your DNA (Previously Aired)." YouTube, 22 Aug. 2015, www.youtube.com/watch?v=XEgwYq31wxk.

Dorsch, Cathie. Confessions for Raising Winning Kids. Tulsa: Harrison House. Print. 1996.

Omartian, Stormie. The Power of a Praying Parent. Eugene: Harvest House Publishers. Print. 1995.

### A Secret Weapon

Hagin, Kenneth E. Seven Vital Steps to Receiving the Holy Spirit.

Tulsa: Faith Library Publications. Print. 1980.

Copeland, Gloria. God's Will is the Holy Spirit. Tulsa: Harrison House; Revised Edition. Print. 2000.

### We Can't Force Seasons

"Ability May Get You to the Top, but It Takes Character to Keep You There." John Wooden: Ability May Get You to the Top, but It Takes Character to Keep You There., Quotes, www.quotes.net/ quote/6555.